❖ ❖ ❖

I WISH SOMEONE
HAD TOLD ME

❖ ❖ ❖

I WISH SOMEONE HAD TOLD ME

✣ ✣ ✣

A Realistic Guide to Early Motherhood

NINA BARRETT

Academy Chicago Publishers

Published in 1997 by
Academy Chicago Publishers
363 West Erie Street
Chicago, Illinois 60610

First paperback edition 1990 by Simon & Schuster

© 1990 by Nina Barrett

Printed and bound in the U.S.A.

Library of Congress Cataloging-in-Publication data

Barrett, Nina.
    I wish someone had told me : a realistic guide to early motherhood
/ Nina Barrett.
    p.   cm.
    Originally published: New York : Simon & Schuster, c1990.
    ISBN 0-89733-422-6
    1. Motherhood—United States. 2. Infants—Care—United States.
3. Mothers—United States—Interviews. I. Title.
HQ759.B285   1997
306.874'3—dc21   97-7795
                                                          CIP

To the people who
taught me about
being a parent:

Rowena and John Barrett

and

Ellis, Sam, and George Booker

acknowledgments

My deepest thanks must go to the sixty-three women who shared their stories with me. I would have thanked them by name had the conversations not often been so intimate.

I would never have found these women without the help of Aviva Rubin, Kathy Cain, Kathy Kahn, Sue Husar, and the Evanston new-mother organization, Mothers in Touch.

Dr. Jeffrey Grabenstein inadvertently got me started when the reading list he scrawled for me on a prescription pad didn't have exactly the book I was looking for; he and Dr. Diane Fabricius also helped us navigate a variety of early-parenting crises.

Dr. Linda Holt and Trisha Woollcott, C.N.M., generously shared their knowledge and experience about recovering from childbirth.

I would also like to thank all the people who helped me shape the material. My sister, Joan Wickersham, was adamant about having women speak for themselves. After reading some of the early chapters, she, Ellen Blum Barish and Deborah Leigh Wood gave me advice and encouragement on an ongoing basis.

Lila Freedman, Cheryl Haigler, and Barbara Anderson taught me lessons in writing and publishing without which I would never have undertaken a project like this.

Finally, I can never sufficiently thank the people who've cared for Sam with the love and respect no money can buy: Kathy and Kris Chen, Sohae Park, and Mary and Noah King.

contents

introduction

When I had my first baby in the spring of 1987, I'd had no realistic experience with motherhood. I'd had no younger sibling, had never baby-sat for anyone under the age of four, and had never even seen a newborn infant. My college buddies hadn't gotten around to childbearing yet, and my classmates in graduate school were intensely focused on their careers.

Nevertheless, I had absorbed certain expectations. From my Lamaze classes, I picked up the idea that an earnest and positive approach to childbirth would foster a pleasant experience. From the Superwoman profiles in the women's magazines, I knew my husband and I would share equally in the child-care burden, while I continued to pursue my career. I don't know where I got that odd idea about babies snoozing peacefully till they were old enough for preschool, but I guess I should have taken a few courses in child development.

At any rate, reality came as a shock. One of my first thoughts after labor was finally over was: "Why didn't anyone tell me that it *hurts!*" Clearly, childhood educators and pregnancy-guide authors preferred to gloss over the degree of pain that could be involved in a fairly normal labor. Unless, I wondered, this hadn't been a "normal" experience.

As the weeks passed and I began to get out of the apartment, I discovered that many other women were wondering the same thing about their labors. Everywhere I went, women with new babies in Snuglis would ask me, "How old is yours?" and then inevitably follow up with, "How was your labor?"

Then these perfect strangers and I would exchange copious details about one of the most intimate experiences of our lives. How long had it lasted? Had we needed drugs? A cesarean? How much had it hurt? Had we screamed?

Then, if the conversation kept on, it would inevitably hit the subject of crying. We were all vaguely familiar with the Spockian concept of the "age of spoiling," granting a sort of three-month amnesty during which we were allowed to pick up our infants at any sign of distress and try to comfort them. But in the fourth month, we were supposed to get tough. Let 'em cry it out. Otherwise, the experts agreed, our babies wouldn't learn good sleep habits or a sense of independence.

We all "knew" this, but no one could quite bear to do it. We'd let them cry a little bit, or maybe even a lot when we were absolutely at the ends of our ropes, but as a matter of policy, we all felt that if the baby could be calmed by our touch, well, wasn't that what we were there for?

Nevertheless, in following our own instincts about what a good mother should do, we felt a nagging guilt at defying the "experts." Just as Lamaze propaganda intimidated us into concluding that our own experiences of childbirth must have been "wrong," so we were intimidated by the pediatricians and child-care authors who told us not to do what we thought we should do, and who presumably had access to the correct, thoroughly researched, and scientifically proven answers to all child-care questions. Furthermore, just as we believed in our own endless capacity for self-improvement, we started out believing that, with the right techniques, we could teach our babies to sleep longer, eat better, and cry less. Only slowly did it begin to occur to us that we could thumb our noses at the experts and say of the baby, "Well, that's just the way he is."

And only slowly did it occur to me that it was these other new mothers—as hesitant and self-doubting as I—rather than the experts, who were really helping me feel comfortable with motherhood. What I sought, I began to realize, wasn't someone else's answers to the questions I was asking, but confirmation that someone else was asking the same questions.

The expectations I had brought to motherhood were collapsing. Clearly, the baby could not be shoved, sleeping peacefully, under my desk while I wrote brilliantly, nor could I bear to send him into full-time child care while I passionately pursued the kind of reporting job I had once thought I wanted. My idea of a "career" would have to be adjusted to accommodate both what the baby demanded of me and what I found myself wanting to try to give him. And clearly, my marriage was not going to follow a classic feminist blueprint of perfect sex-role equality, even though that's what I had always fiercely believed in.

Most importantly, I was not, as I'd imagined I would be, always in control. Pregnancy, labor, and breast-feeding taught me what miracles my body could perform without input from my intellect. The baby taught me how futile it could be to try to impose my will on his natural course of development. I wouldn't sleep regularly again until he did, and I wouldn't be able to work well again until I began to get sleep. I wouldn't have my old body back until I regained the time, energy, and self-discipline for diet and exercise—and I couldn't wear any of those old "dry-clean-only" clothes anyway until the spitting-up phase had passed.

In short, I discovered that after giving birth to a baby, I was having to give birth to a new self, and that the process, like labor, was longer, more complicated, and much more painful than any of the books indicated. Just as my body had stretched and ached to bear this child, so my whole life—my relationships, my ambitions, and my self-image—would have to rework itself around the baby's presence.

Some women make this transition effortlessly, just as some women have easy labors. For those of us who aren't so fortunate, though, there's no magic technique or formula that can make the process shorter or more pleasant. But there is a certain solace in knowing you have company in the struggle.

I began writing this book to try to capture the sort of comfort I got from talking to other new mothers about what we were going through. In all, I interviewed sixty-three women, most of them at some stage of their first year of motherhood, some as early as the first few weeks. The interviews were open-ended, lasting between half an hour and three hours, with the majority lasting around two. I found the women through childbirth-preparation classes, new mothers' groups, newspaper advertisements, and word-of-mouth. Many of them talked to me about the most intimate aspects of their feelings and relationships with wrenching honesty, and I have guarded their privacy by changing their names and their children's names, and, in some cases, other details that might identify them.

I have used the material from these interviews anecdotally, not sociologically. It was never my ambition to formulate theories about how the average woman experiences motherhood, or even to write the sort of neutral, universalized text so many child-care books feature with the hope of sounding applicable to every potential reader.

On the contrary, I've tried to pinpoint those aspects of childbearing and early motherhood that seemed most controversial, emotionally loaded, or problematic to the women I interviewed. I've offered some of my own advice and passed on some of the advice the women gave me, but for the most part, I've used interview material to demonstrate how many different ways there are of approaching these subjects. And I've used historical material to show how much "expert" opinion on many of these subjects has flip-flopped over time.

Most of all, I hope this book serves as an antidote to the

Superwoman myth, which so many women intellectually reject but emotionally still judge themselves by. Self-confidence is perhaps the most important prerequisite for enjoying motherhood, and it's hard to develop when you suspect that everyone else out there is doing a much better job of holding life together than you are. The secret I discovered while researching this book is that *no one knows the secret:* we are each putting our motherhood together from scratch.

one

Ideal *Labor should be painless, natural, and emotionally fulfilling.*

Fact *Labor can be unbearably painful, medically assisted, and emotionally traumatic.*

Y ou bought the pregnancy books. In your last and longest month, you read the chapters on labor over and over, wondering whether you'd recognize a contraction when you had one or whether you'd be one of those lucky women who does most of her dilating in her sleep.

You did Lamaze, attending classes religiously, reading the handouts, practicing the breathing at home. You overcame your squeamishness and kept your eyes open during the birth movie; you cried when the head crowned. You toured the hospital.

In short, you were as prepared for birth as anyone could ever be. If labor had been a final exam, you would have aced the course.

Perhaps you did. Your labor progressed pretty much as you expected, with a degree of pain you found perfectly manageable, or no pain at all. You may have wondered what all the fuss was about.

But perhaps you feel you blew it. You went through hell. You lost control. You yelled at your husband or threw up on a nurse or screamed and screamed or accepted a painkiller or needed forceps or ended up with a cesarean. Or all of the above.

If that was the case, it's not unusual to emerge from the delivery room feeling shocked, embarrassed, guilty, betrayed, and disappointed in yourself. "Why didn't anyone *tell* me it could be like that?" you think one moment, and the next, "Was it supposed to be like that, or did something go really wrong?"

The fact is, not only is it possible to do all your reading and studying and practicing and *still* not be prepared for the reality of labor, it's possible that all the reading and studying actually set you up with unrealistic expectations about labor. Today, women get much of their information from advocates of a particular technique of childbirth, who tend to present drug-free, intervention-free, painless labor as the goal all women should aspire to.

Unfortunately, as a quick look back through history shows, this is merely the newest utopian vision in a long line of fads dictating what a woman's labor *should* be like. And all these visions—of births painful and painless, drugged and undrugged—have been promoted by their advocates as the most "natural" method.

In the Beginning

Many childbirth writers insist on a scenario in which our uncivilized ancestors had an "intuitive" knowledge of the childbirth process, allowing them to give birth "naturally," without pain or fuss. But since our ancestors didn't leave memoirs, it's a hard theory to prove.

However, we do know that as far back as the fifth century B.C.

the Greek playwright Euripides gave his character Medea the comment: "They say that we lead a life without danger at home, while the men go to war—but they are wrong: I would rather stand in the hoplite ranks three times than give birth once."

And the writers of the Old Testament had seen enough childbirth agony to feel compelled to explain its origins—in Eve's bite of apple. "In sorrow thou shalt bring forth children," God proclaims in Genesis, implying that not only is the pain "natural," women deserve it.

This biblical attitude sailed into America with the Puritans, and women continued to redeem their sins with suffering. Wrote one nineteenth-century mother, "I went down to death's door to bring my son into the world, and I've never forgotten. Some folks say one forgets, and can have them right over again, but today I've not forgotten, and that baby is thirty-six years old."

Then, in the mid-1800s, medical science stumbled upon anesthesia, which was immediately adopted for surgical use and was shown to reduce labor pain. But an enormous debate ensued among "experts" of the day who felt that anything used to reduce pain in childbirth was undesirable because it was "unnatural." In *Pain, Pleasure and American Childbirth*, Margarete Sandelowski writes that many clergymen denounced anesthesia for interfering with the divine will that women suffer. Doctors, meanwhile, worried that "childbirth pain was necessary to the physiological course of labor, to act as a cuing device for physicians in the proper management of labor, to the development of normal female emotions, and to the establishment of a healthy mother-infant bond."

But by the 1920s, Sandelowski writes, attitudes were completely reversed. Convinced that childbirth pain and its anticipation interfered with the ideal experience of pregnancy and motherhood, women flocked to doctors who offered them Twilight Sleep. This was a combination of drugs that induced semiconsciousness during labor, allowing the woman to feel pain but not to remember it afterward. One doctor gushed that

Twilight Sleep restored "the truly *natural* conditions of birth by allowing a woman's natural reflexes to predominate" (emphasis mine).

The pendulum swung back again in the 1940s, when a book by the British obstetrician Grantly Dick-Read called *Natural Child-birth* (in later editions, *Childbirth Without Fear*) helped spark a popular rebellion against anesthesia. Dick-Read was a profoundly religious man who did not believe God could have intended a process as miraculous as childbirth to hurt women. Pain, he argued, was a direct result of the fear and tension surrounding labor in the civilized world. Educated about the facts of labor and supported by a doctor or midwife who believed in his method, he said, at least 95 percent of women would have drug-free, pain-free birth, the way "nature" had intended.

The French obstetrician Fernand Lamaze agreed with Dick-Read that pain in labor was caused by fear and tension. Basing his theories on Pavlov's experiments with dogs (Psych. 101: dogs who naturally salivated when food was present were conditioned to salivate at the sound of the bell that signaled the food), Lamaze argued that a woman who was conditioned by his breathing and relaxation techniques could control her responses during labor and eliminate pain. When Marjorie Karmel, who popularized Lamaze in America with her 1959 book, *Thank You, Dr. Lamaze*, first went to Lamaze's assistant to learn the techniques, she was told that the system was *not* called "natural" childbirth because "the final result should be better than nature."

Ironically, today Lamaze's name is synonymous with "natural" childbirth. The birth-preparation classes that bear his name consist, for the most part, of his conditioning techniques watered down to a level at which they hardly constitute conditioning and are mixed with bits and pieces of other childbirth philosophies. These classes also usually attempt to prepare you for hospital birthing practices—which are often in direct contradiction to the "natural" childbirth principles.

The result is an "education" that may have left you with a

jumble of expectations and hopes about birth which were sadly removed from reality.

When You Can't Get Over Your Labor

This section is not for or about those women who *do* have painless or bearably painful labors, nor is it intended to argue that such labors don't happen. What it is meant to do is to provide an antidote to all the "reassuring" material about labor you'll find in most pregnancy and birth guides, for those women who think their "birth experience" ran amok and wonder if they're to blame.

If you and your baby both emerged safely from the delivery room, but you can't shake the feeling that something went wrong, consider the expectations you went in with, where you got them from, and whether they were reasonable in the first place.

▪ *"I Read and I Took Classes, So I Should Have Been Prepared."* All those years in school have convinced most of us that doing our homework pays off; and in school, it does. But majoring in political science doesn't prepare you to be president any more than watching a swim meet prepares you to swim the English Channel. For labor, there is no real preparation other than having gone through it before. Even obstetricians and nurses who deal with childbirth on a daily basis have no advantage.

> I was an obstetrical nurse before I had the baby, so I figured I was an expert. I had seen women screaming hysterically in labor, but the other nurses told me those were the wimps. For myself, I assumed Lamaze would take care of everything, that I'd just sit back and take a few breaths and everything would be fine.

But I learned that when people talk about pain—even when they watch women in pain, as I had—they just can't comprehend the type of pain it is. I got my contractions in couplets, with no relief in between. And I was only at 3 or 4 centimeters when I couldn't stand it anymore and asked for drugs.

It took me three or four months of comparing my labor story with other women to make me feel I'd done "okay." Even though my nursing background had convinced me that the medication wasn't a problem for the baby, Lamaze had really put down drugs. So I ended up feeling like a wimp.

There was a female obstetrician who had a baby at the hospital where I worked. I'd seen her with patients and she wasn't particularly sympathetic when women got upset during delivery. But she herself was screaming and totally out of control at 3 centimeters. So it just goes to show, you can know it all, and still not have a good labor.

■ *"I Thought I'd Have an Easy Time."*   A favorite image among pregnant women is that of the hearty peasant who squats in a corner of the field to give birth, then plops the infant into a shoulder sling and goes back to hoeing the ground. That same little mechanism that pumps hope eternally into the human breast convinces many of us that we'll be like that peasant woman.

It's hard not to hear labor horror stories, even when you're pregnant, but many of us manage to hear them without listening to them. And most of what we hear and read during pregnancy is quite consciously presented in a "nonthreatening" way, since many experts believe fear increases the pain of childbirth. And because most of this material also implies that we have control over and responsibility for our labor (a debatable assumption), it's quite natural to assume we'll do as good a job at it as we do in all the other areas of our lives.

I have an hourglass shape, and my husband always used to say that my body was built for childbearing. It was sort of a joke between us, but somewhere deep inside I really believed it. After twenty-one horrible hours of labor, the doctor finally pried the baby out of me with forceps.

On the first day of my Lamaze class, the teacher looked around the room and said, "The statistics indicate that at least one of you is going to have a cesarean." I remember feeling sorry for that poor person. It never occurred to me that it would be me.

■ *"I Underestimated the Pain."* It's hard not to underestimate, since all we have to go on is the memory of pain we've suffered in the past—cramps, headaches, backaches, dental work. But the intensity and duration of labor pain is hard to predict. Some women say they honestly didn't feel anything they would describe as pain, while others emerge from the experience happy to be alive and determined never to go through it again. Some women say their contractions felt like menstrual cramps; other describe feeling as though their stomachs were about to explode.

At the same time, your manuals and childbirth education teacher may have ignored or denied the reality of pain in childbirth. Grantly Dick-Read, one of the earliest natural childbirth enthusiasts (and, like many childbirth "experts," a man), believed that fear of pain was a direct cause of pain for laboring women. If women were not conditioned to expect labor to be painful, he argued, then with some prenatal education and a lot of support from birth attendants, they wouldn't suffer pain. So, to this day, natural childbirth advocates deliberately airbrush their language, referring neutrally to "powerful sensations" and "hard work."

Clearly, no one wants to terrorize legions of unsuspecting pregnant women. But if you went through that stage said to be characterized by "some discomfort" in mortal agony, the problem is not that you overreacted. You felt what you felt, and the majority of laboring women feel like that, too. (See box: Does Prepared Childbirth Work?)

Does Prepared Childbirth Work?

If you took what is loosely referred to as a Lamaze or Prep-aration for Birth class, your instruction was based on the the-ory that childbirth *can* be but doesn't necessarily *have* to be painful.

Despite the proliferation of books with titles like *Painless Childbirth* and *Overcoming Labor Pain,* no independent research has ever substantiated such claims. A 1949 study of 400 women attempting prepared natural childbirth at Yale–New Haven Hospital reported that only 2 percent found labor "painless." And a 1954 report on 2,000 prepared women found that 66 percent required drugs in the first stage of labor (dilatation), while 71 percent required them in the second (pushing) stage.

In 1981, a team of Canadian researchers measured the level of pain experienced by 141 prepared and unprepared women laboring at Montreal General Hospital. They found that although the prepared women reported a slightly lower level of pain, 81 percent still requested an epidural—as com-pared to 82 percent of the unprepared women.

"These results show that the title of Lamaze's book, *Painless Childbirth,* is misleading," the researchers concluded. "Al-though the pain is diminished, the reduction is not nearly as large as the title suggests."*

* From "Labour Is Still Painful After Prepared Childbirth Training," *Canadian Medical Association Journal,* Vol. 125, 1981, pp. 357–363.

The terms used in parents' classes should be those they may hear used in the hospital. Commonly, the term *medication* refers to analgesics and tranquilizers; terms such as *painkiller* should be avoided because they have a negative connotation.

—*Textbook for Childbirth Educators.*

What to Do if Your Labor Was Traumatic

1. *Talk about It with Anyone Who Will Listen.* You've been through something enormously significant, and you're still trying to make sense of it. Your husband or labor coach can fill you in on things you didn't notice or forgot and can continue to give emotional support long after the event has passed. Talking to your obstetrician, midwife, or childbirth education teacher may also help. Unfortunately, many women find their feelings are so negative that they're afraid to confront any of these professionals. Actually, the more negative your feelings, the more good it would probably do to force yourself. You may get some explanation that will put your mind at ease. And if you feel some lapse on their part was really damaging to you, you may be doing some other expectant woman a big favor by mentioning it.

Talking to other women is an age-old balm for the newly delivered. Finally, you're really *interested* in the kind of horror stories you tried to fend off during pregnancy. Things could have been worse, you learn. Or perhaps yours is the worst story you've ever heard: Pat yourself on the back for how well you did under the circumstances.

2. *Write It Down in as Much Detail as You Can, with Your Feelings Included.* Getting something on paper often helps free the mind. And, although you don't believe it now, the memory will eventually fade. After the horror evaporates, you may actually look back with pride on what you've done.

3. *Read about It.* This may be the best way of getting your factual questions answered—the questions you didn't know enough to ask before the birth. And it may help you think about the arrangements you'll want to make next time around, if there is a next time.

- *"I Overestimated My Control over the Pain."* There are several good reasons you may have done this. The first, if you took a Lamaze class, is that you were exposed to breathing and relaxation techniques which, you were told, would enable you to "stay on top" of your contractions.

Aside from the question of whether these techniques actually work when taught the way Dr. Lamaze intended them to be taught, the fact is that in America they rarely *are* taught the way he intended them to be taught, nor are women who labor in most hospitals given the support Lamaze made sure his patients had. Six evenings of lectures about stages of labor and degrees of dilatation do not produce the level of conditioning required to discipline the body into automatic response. It is interesting to note that various studies of American and Canadian women who've taken Lamaze classes have shown that, although they described their labors as slightly less painful than women without the preparation, between 80 and 90 percent still requested some form of pain medication.

That leads us to the second reason. You probably assumed that if things got really bad, you'd just take the drugs and feel better. But many so-called "painkillers" don't actually kill the pain; they simply make you too relaxed, tired, or limp to really care about it. Even epidurals can fail to take.

- *"I Overestimated My Control over Myself."* All of us know in our hearts what beautiful movie heroines do when captured by the Gestapo and tortured for their secrets: No matter what happens, they remain tight-lipped and beautiful—just as the heroines of Lamaze films do. Under similar circumstances, we hope we'd behave the same way.

Whether you went into labor confident or fearful, you may have been shocked at what you became capable of while in extreme pain. You found yourself moaning, crying out, screaming bloody murder, swearing, or thrashing. Perhaps, God forbid, you were even *rude* to the resident who decided to conduct an internal exam at the height of your contraction.

After the birth, or perhaps even between the contractions, you were ashamed of how you acted, and you apologized right and left.

You have nothing to be ashamed of. Until someone *does* find a universally effective and safe cure for labor pain, many women will continue to experience agony that few men have ever known. If you are still worrying about what the doctor, the nurses, or your husband thought of your behavior, remember that they had the easy part of the job.

> My most vivid memory of labor is of being pushed down the hall on a gurney from the labor room to the delivery room, screaming my guts out at every contraction. It felt like the only thing I *could* do with that kind of pain. It even felt good, in a way. But then, between the contractions, I was thinking, "Oh my, I hope all the women in the early stages have their doors closed. I don't want to scare them about what's coming." Also, I kept apologizing to the people around me. Here I was, in front of complete strangers, making an incredible scene.

■ *"I Overestimated My Control over the Process."* Aside from your feelings about how you behaved under the stress and pain of labor, you may also worry about the decisions you made—and about those that turned out to be out of your hands.

Perhaps you accepted medication even though you knew there was some risk involved for the baby. Perhaps you pictured yourself squatting through the contractions to take advantage of gravity, but instead found yourself wired up like a switchboard and flat on your back.

Or maybe you're now second-guessing the need for your cesarean, or forceps delivery. You know that the doctor must have had safety uppermost in his or her mind, but you also wonder how everything could have gone so wrong.

The problem is that you are caught between the rock and the hard place of modern childbirth. You have absorbed your expectations about labor from a natural childbirth movement which preaches that women *should* have control over their labors, but you delivered in a hospital where, in fact, doctors and medical staff *do* have control.

The fact is that you were not in a very good position to make all those decisions you understood responsible, intelligent women should make about their own deliveries. For one thing, unlike the sources of much of your advice, you had never been through it before. You didn't know what a contraction felt like, you didn't know how you'd react to pain, you didn't know whether the hospital staff would be friendly and comforting or coldly professional, and you didn't know what an episiotomy would feel like as it healed.

By the time you had some personal familiarity with the subject, you were in an even worse position. You were in pain, or you were extremely worried about the baby, and your husband, who was supposed to be your clear-eyed advocate in all this, was worried about both of you and just wanted it to be over.

And finally, the fact is that your doctor or midwife and the hospital staff controlled the way your labor was handled. If no serious physical damage was done to you, but you still aren't happy with the way you were treated, the most you can do at this point is to complain. And you can also start thinking about what sort of arrangements you'll want to make next time around.

■ *"I Didn't Find the Birth Emotionally Fulfilling."*   Once upon a time, the measure of a successful birth was whether the mother and the baby survived. But with the resurgence of "natural" childbirth, spearheaded by Grantly Dick-Read, our standards were raised considerably.

Not only would a fearless woman give birth painlessly, Dick-Read claimed, but for her the experience would be euphoric, profoundly religious, and a complete satisfaction of her "highest ambition." Other writers (often male) have embellished this theme.

If your main response to childbirth was relief that it was over, this does not brand you as a shallow and self-centered woman who is incapable of appreciating the Mystery of Birth. Remember, it takes a certain amount of energy to feel elated—the kind of energy that observers of a birth tend to retain after watching a delivery but which the woman who has actually given birth may not have.

This attitude is exemplified by Leni Schwartz in her 1980 book, *The World of the Unborn,* in which she says that giving birth "can be can be a window to intrinsic patterns of the universe, to cycles of life and death that have existed since the first matter crossed the indefinable line and took the form of living cells. One transcends the ordinary, familiar sense of self to achieve an extraordinary understanding of being one with the cosmos. Women sense their autonomy, at the same time they experience being part of all that is, ever has been, ever will be."

I was in labor, start to finish, for five hours. For the first two hours, I wasn't even sure what it was. While my husband called the doctor, I got into the shower to shampoo my hair. We went to the hospital, and I had him about an hour and a half later.

It wasn't bad. I didn't need any drugs. I don't really remember it as being uncomfortable, although I do remember holding my husband's wrist so hard I thought it was going to break.

But I wasn't thinking to myself, "Oh, the Miracle of Birth, it's all worth it." Quite honestly, the first thing I wanted was food. I was starving. They said, "Do you want to see the baby?" And I said, "I want breakfast."

Recommended Reading

Immaculate Deception II: A Fresh Look at Childbirth by Suzanne Arms. Celestial Arts, Berkeley, Calif., 1994.

Lying-In: A History of Childbirth in America by Richard W. and Dorothy C. Wertz. Yale University Press, New Haven, 1989.

Pain, Pleasure and American Childbirth: From the Twilight Sleep to the Read Method, 1914–1960 by Margarete Sandelowski. Greenwood Press, Westport, Conn., 1984.

Rebounding From Childbirth: Toward Emotional Recovery by Lynn Masden. Bergin & Garvey, Westport, Conn., 1994.

Old Wives' Tales

Yes, Those Quick-and-Easy First Labors Really Do Happen

My water broke at 3:30 in the morning. I went to the hospital at 7:00 A.M., and by then my contractions were ninety seconds long. So I was already pretty far along.

But it wasn't hurting. It felt like a wave of pressure that would start in my back, linger, and go away. It felt like someone pushing a little bit on my back.

When I got to the hospital, the doctor found that I was 7 centimeters dilated. "You look so calm, I thought you were going to be at two!" he told me. Only maybe for the last three contractions before I got to 10 centimeters would I say it kind of hurt. And even then, it didn't *really* hurt—it's just that it lasted so long that it got kind of uncomfortable. I had a crown put on my tooth that I thought was a lot more painful.

The baby was born at 10:30 A.M.

I was glad I took Lamaze, because I couldn't imagine going through it not knowing what was going to happen next. But I didn't need any of the breathing.

I was surprised by how much it hurt afterwards, by how sore my bottom was. I was so afraid to go to the bathroom.

A Routine Hospital Birth

Two days before my due date, I leaked some fluid, so we'd gone to the hospital to get me checked. The medical student told me I was 4 centimeters dilated, and that my husband and I should go out and walk around and see if I progressed. So I went out, and came back, and the med student examined me again, and then she asked the resident to examine me, and the resident said, "You're not at four, you're at one." So they sent me home. And I was really upset.

The next night, at about 9:00, I felt something almost like a menstrual cramp, but I could tell by the way it seemed to move across from my back to my front that I was in labor. My husband was working late, and when he got home, I told him, "Something may be happening, but I'm not sure, so let's just wait and see." I knew this was the real thing, but I just didn't want to go through what I'd gone through the day before.

Around 1:00 A.M., I told him to get a little sleep, because I had a feeling he'd need it. By 3:30, I was getting very uncomfortable, I couldn't lie down anymore; I had to move around. Then I noticed that I was losing fluid down my legs, and I thought that was as good a sign as I was going to get. So I called the hospital, and they said, "Come on in, and we'll evaluate you."

So we got there at about 4:00 A.M., and they said I was in labor, and was about 4 centimeters dilated. By this point, the contractions felt as though I had a metal belt around my middle, and someone was tightening and then loosening it. It was uncomfortable, but it wasn't what I would describe as really painful.

They told me I didn't have to be on a monitor yet, that I could walk around. I wasn't too keen on it, but my husband thought it would be a good idea, so we did that for an hour or so. But by about 7:00 A.M. I'd had enough; whenever I got a contraction, I was having to stop and just lean against a wall and do the breathing.

So we went back to Labor and Delivery, and they put me in a bed with a monitor on, and for the next nine hours I pretty much lay there and dozed between the contractions. My husband slept in the chair next to me. The TV was on, and I have this sort of surreal memory of laboring by *Leave It to Beaver*. The contractions were about four minutes apart, and they stayed at about the same intensity; they weren't getting any more intense.

Around 2:00 in the afternoon, the doctor came in, looked at me, and said, "Well, you're leaking, but the bag hasn't broken yet. Rather than give you Pitocin, why don't we just break the bag and see if that speeds things up." So she broke the bag. And immediately after she broke the bag, the contractions became much more intense. They were verging on being too uncomfortable to take. I did take it for about forty-five minutes, but then I asked for a painkiller. But then they had to find an IV nurse because I don't like shots, and that took probably twenty minutes.

Meanwhile, the doctor examined me and found that I was at 9 centimeters. She said, "You know, it might not be worth it to do it now, you're so close." But finally they decided I could have some Dilaudid.

And after that, I just watched the flowers march up the wallpaper. At one point, I turned to my husband and said, "I'm as high as a kite." It just took enough of an edge off it so I didn't feel like I wanted to yell.

About 4:00 P.M. the doctor asked if I felt like I wanted to push. I said no. She said, "Well, you let us know when that happens." And that was odd, because I couldn't imagine what that was going to feel like, but then about fifteen minutes went by, and I could feel my body telling me it was time. It was that same feeling you get when you're going to have a bowel movement. But then they told me I was still only at 9 centimeters, and I couldn't push. That was tough. The breathing really helped with that.

Then, about fifteen minutes later, they told me to go ahead. The Dilaudid was wearing off. I was feeling quite lucid. The pushing was extremely difficult work, but not really painful. When you're not in labor, you think, "I should be careful, maybe I could damage myself." When you are in labor, you're thinking, "I have to do this, I have to do this," and you're not thinking of anything else. It was a feeling of needing badly to get rid of something. It was a very urgent feeling.

After each push, I felt completely exhausted. And my whole body started shivering and shaking. That was difficult to deal with.

I pushed for about forty-five minutes, and then they took me to the delivery room. Then it was about another twenty minutes. The doctor was about to do the episiotomy—in fact, she had the scissors in place—when the head just popped out. I tore slightly.

They hadn't had time to set everything up, so there was no mirror to watch in. And I don't think I really wanted to, anyway. I could tell everything that was happening by how it felt. When the skin was stretching to let the baby's head out, I could feel a very intense, burning sensation.

My husband cut the cord. As soon as she was delivered, I was immediately wide awake. The first thing I said was that I was hungry and I wanted something to eat.

Another Routine Hospital Birth

I'm someone who reads a lot and asks a lot of questions, and I took a Lamaze class. So I was surprised at how surprised I was about the physical and emotional intensity of labor. I had thought, "I'm so prepared, *nothing* can bowl me over." But I felt bowled over.

At 4:07 on the afternoon before my due date, I was taking a nap and I started to feel these light, cramping sensations. Almost whimsically, I decided to time them. They were coming at ten- or fifteen-minute intervals. For the first hour, I kept answering phone calls and just chatting my way through the contractions. It made me feel high, to be in labor and to be able to laugh and talk like that.

Then I called my husband and told him to come home from work. And from 6:00 P.M. till about 10:00 P.M., I'd say it was still very pleasant. The contractions were closer together, maybe four to six minutes apart. I ate a bit, and we took a walk around 8:30. I was so elated—I thought, "Well, if it's going to be like this, I can handle it fine!"

Around 10:30 P.M., we thought we should go to the hospital. When they examined me, I was 3 centimeters dilated. They also told us that all the rooms were full and we should walk around for a while, which we did. That seemed to really get things going. The contractions started to get painful, and I had to sit down and use the Lamaze breathing for each one. I was definitely getting uncomfortable.

At about 1:00 in the morning, I went into the ladies' room and ran into another laboring woman I'd seen walking around the hospital with her husband. We smiled at each other, and I said, "How's it going?" And she said, "Well, this is my twenty-second hour." And she was *still* walking around!

That seemed like a bad omen. Till then, labor had seemed quite tolerable. I'd been joking with the nurses, and they were teasing me because I'd told them how I do a lot of yoga and consider myself quite fit, and how I'd pictured myself being able to birth this baby squatting. They said, "Sure, honey." And I laughed with them, but I was also kind of wondering if they knew something I didn't know.

At about 1:30 or 2:00 A.M., they got me a room. I was 7 centimeters dilated, and the contractions were coming so close that I couldn't rest in between. Then they decided that I needed to be put onto an IV. I was upset about it, and it seemed to slow things down. And I was in so much pain, I just felt I couldn't stand it anymore, so they gave me some Dilaudid, which really took the edge off.

But it surprised me how much of the time I was left alone with my husband. I hadn't realized that the doctor wouldn't show up till the very end. And the nursing staff seemed to be spread very thin, with only one nurse to every three or four laboring women. I got the sense that I wasn't being examined as much as I should have been. At one point, I told them I was feeling the urge to push, but no one came in to check me. I think I may actually have been completely dilated for an hour and a half, trying very hard not to push, before anyone came and checked.

Then, at about 8:00 in the morning, they finally told me I could push. But I couldn't figure out how. My lower back was incredibly sore, and my legs were up, and I was gripping the sides of the bed, and I had no idea *what* to push. I had no strength left and I couldn't understand how to combine the breathing with the pushing. It was very, very painful. It felt like a bowel movement that was lodged way, way up there. I guess I had thought it would be more like a regular bowel movement that you could just excrete. But this just wouldn't budge. I had to move it, centimeter by centimeter.

They offered to let me watch in the mirror, but I just couldn't. I was afraid it would make me lose the concentration on my breathing. And I was also kind of scared to see what it looked like down there, with the episiotomy and everything.

When she came out, she was very blue, which was scary. I felt joy, but I think I was also in shock. I didn't feel I was bonding with her, exactly. But they let me nurse her, and I was heartened that she had a very nice sucking reflex. She basically taught me how to nurse her, and I thought, "Wow, this little child knows how to do this, and I don't."

But my husband seemed to feel this instant connection to her, which I couldn't understand. He was so happy. Ultimately, it took me a lot longer to feel what he seemed to feel, even though the mother is supposedly closer to the baby.

The next day, I was consumed with reliving the whole labor. I wanted my husband to do a blow-by-blow, but he didn't seem interested. He was so happy at the result that he just seemed able to forget what we'd gone through. But I really needed to talk about it.

So I talked a lot to my roommates. One wasn't that chatty, and the other one was *very* negative. She said she would *never* go through it again, and she didn't want to breast-feed, and she was completely bowled over by the experience. And the woman I'd run into in the bathroom had ended up having a thirty-eight-hour labor.

Initially, I was pretty shocked at my own experience, but talking to these women made me think, "At least mine wasn't *that* bad!" Still, I'm surprised by how much it hurt and by how I handled it. I mean, in my right mind I know I handled it fine, but I was out of control. My husband keeps telling me, "You were great; you were an athlete." But you know, it wasn't my fantasy of childbirth, even though it was vaginal and there were very few drugs.

I'm still wondering how I could have made it more ideal. I'm questioning whether the IV slowed the process, whether I gave in to things I shouldn't have, what effect the Dilaudid had on the baby, why I needed the episiotomy. I feel haunted by certain parts of it. And I think next time—if there is a next time—I'll have a midwife so there's someone there all the time who understands what I'm going through.

The day afterward, I was sure I'd never go through it again. Now, I feel more positive, but still hesitant.

I'd like to let a lot of time pass.

A "Hell-on-Earth" Labor, with Epidural and Forceps

I thought I was really into the aesthetics of childbirth. I bought Bach tapes and made this book with comments from all my friends that I was going to read in the delivery room. I brought along postcards from the art museum. I even asked if I could bring in my parakeets. I expected it to be really beautiful.

Of course, I'd had moments of dread, too, just because of the way women always seemed to roll their eyes when they talked about it. And just the pure physics of the situation—getting such a big baby through this tiny vaginal opening—seemed inherently troubling.

Well, in labor, my body went totally haywire. I woke up at 5:00 A.M. with contractions that were fifteen minutes apart, and after three contractions, they were down to five-minute intervals. I vomited ten times before I could even call the midwife. She said to get into a warm bath to relax, and apparently my water bag broke in the tub, because all of a sudden the contractions were coming every minute.

We knew we had to get to the hospital fast, but my husband

couldn't get me into the car. The contractions were coming so fast and so hard that I just kept collapsing on the floor. I couldn't get myself dressed, he couldn't carry me, and I couldn't walk. I collapsed onto the couch, then I got up and fell onto the floor.

Meanwhile, my husband went into a complete tailspin and started yelling at me, "Get up off the floor; walk around a little!" Because that's what he'd heard in Lamaze class: "Have her walk around. Give her a cup of tea." But I was way past that stage of labor already, and I was in excruciating pain.

The midwife couldn't believe how fast it was happening. The first time I called her, she asked me to come into her office. I told her I couldn't. "Then call me back in an hour," she said. When I called her back, I told her, "Look, I *have* to go to the hospital; I *know* I do." And she said, "Okay, how about if I meet you there in two hours." "You don't understand," I said. "I'm having this baby *now.*"

Finally, in a one-minute break between contractions, I hurled myself out the door and into the car. I didn't even get my winter coat on. I rode on all fours in the front seat, and my husband, who'd had his driver's license for all of two weeks, just sped me to the hospital. I was in mortal agony.

When I got there, they said, "Eight centimeters—that's fantastic! This is going to be a nice, short labor." I felt great about the progress. They put me in a room, and the other 2 centimeters went really fast. The contractions were coming one on top of another. They told me I could start to push. I didn't really feel any urge to push, but they said it was time, so I tried.

And that's when the absolute purgatory began. I pushed for three hours, and the baby never descended even a centimeter. After an hour and a half or so, the midwife and the nurses started looking less upbeat. They said that the baby was fine but must have a billiard-ball head because it just wasn't molding, and they attached a fetal monitor.

So I went for another half hour, and then they decided to put in another monitor to see whether the contractions were "sufficient." So now I was completely wired, with things coming out of every orifice. And I was completely exhausted.

I'd wanted to have pain medication postponed as much as possible. I was afraid of the effects on the baby, and I wanted to use my own musculature if I could. And we kept thinking that it was probably too late, that the birth was imminent. But now I started suggesting that it might be time for some intervention.

Finally, the midwife put her hand all the way up inside me and announced that she didn't think the baby would have trouble fitting through, but that I did have a slight protrusion of the pubic bone, and that therefore the baby's head might need to be guided over the bump. And if it couldn't get over the bump, I would need a cesarean.

So they gave me an epidural and then pulled her out with mid-forceps. But apparently, the episiotomy only allowed her head out, and the rest of her body was stuck. So they gave me a second episiotomy.

I felt as though I were in active combat. It wasn't until the last half hour—till after the epidural—that I had any sense at all of the reality of the baby, that there would be a new baby at the end of all this. While they were getting me ready for the forceps, there was a cesarean delivery going on in the next room. And when I heard the baby crying, tears of joy came to my eyes, because I realized that I was going to have a real, live baby in my arms, too. That's what kept me going.

I don't at all regret the epidural. I don't think there's anything ennobling about pain, and what's the twentieth century for if not to relieve us of pain we don't have to suffer? The thing is, before I went through it, I thought I was being sold a bill of goods about the pain. I thought that if I were just emotionally and physically prepared enough, it wouldn't be as painful as everyone said.

And then I'd heard people comparing it to menstrual cramps, which I've never found particularly unbearable. But it was a totally different order of pain. By the end, if they had wanted to do a cesarean, I'd have said, "Go ahead and do it," and I wouldn't have had any remorse or any feeling that somehow I'd missed part of the "birth experience."

For the whole recovery period—the first six to eight weeks—I had the most intense flashbacks, just the way Vietnam veterans do. They were so emotionally traumatic, I thought I would never, ever have another baby again. I just cowered in terror at the thought that in six months maybe my husband would start to hint around that we should have another baby. I thought, "No one could ever make me go through that again."

But it's been three months now, and it's beginning to fade. The pain, as horrible as it is, goes away. And the joy stays. And that's the only thing that really compensates for the pain: It's finite, while the joy of the baby lasts on and on.

An Emergency Cesarean

I was really psyched up for labor. I wanted to keep it as drug free as possible. I read a lot of books and took a Lamaze class, so of course I had heard some things about C-sections. But somehow it never really occurred to me that it would happen to me.

I was in labor for a long time: four or five hours at home, and then fourteen hours in the hospital. What happened was that the baby's feet got tangled in the cord, so as I kept dilating, his head wasn't dropping. Then I got to 8 centimeters and I wasn't getting any further. The doctor said that normally the head is down further and that helps you get those last few centimeters. But the head wasn't dropping. So they put an internal monitor onto the baby. I was having intense contractions, and his heart rate was dropping.

They gave me an epidural because I'd been stuck in hard labor for four hours and was really exhausted. They thought maybe I could get a rest and relax enough to dilate to 10 centimeters. So they let me go for an hour, but then they got worried about the baby's heart rate. The doctor said, "It doesn't look that good, and I'm worried that the baby is just getting buffeted and beaten by the contractions and just can't move. He's starting to show signs of early distress, and I'd rather move now when it's early than wait and have a real problem."

I was exhausted. I wasn't going to say, "Oh, no, let's keep the baby in there for another hour and see what happens." So I said, "Whatever you have to do." I thought the doctor had been trying so hard *not* to do a C-section that I didn't question the necessity of it at all. But it was scary to be facing this, all of a sudden, without having given it any thought. To be that tired, and to be that far along in the process, and then to hear that the baby's having any kind of problem, is pretty distressing.

Also, at this point my husband was out of the room calling our parents. When he'd left, everything seemed to be proceeding just fine. But then he walked back in, and there I was with an oxygen mask over my face and an anesthesiologist bending over me. And the hospital has a policy that the husband can't be present while they're prepping you for the surgery, so they rolled me out and left him there alone in that totally empty room. He was very freaked out.

Then they got me all hooked up and my husband came in to be with me for the birth. But it was a very weird experience.

For one thing, there was a vaginal birth going on in the room next to me. I could hear them all yelling "PUSH PUSH PUSH" and the woman was really screaming, and even so, I kept thinking enviously, "She's going through that, and I'm not."

They got the baby out very quickly, in just three or four minutes. But for some reason, my arms were shaking uncontrollably, so I couldn't hold him immediately. My husband did, and that was nice. But I'd had this whole image of giving birth to the baby and holding him immediately.

I feel almost like a failure, because I couldn't deliver this baby myself. I know rationally that that's silly. I know that if this had been a hundred years ago, the baby probably would have died unless he'd been lucky enough to get himself untangled. Yet, I still have a nagging sense that if I'd done something differently, I could have had this baby the regular way. And when I hear other women talk about their labor experiences, and they describe the pushing stage, I feel like I missed something because I didn't go through that. I know it's crazy. But I feel like I didn't quite *do* it.

And I know I'll be more nervous going into the next labor because I'll wonder how long I should let myself suffer through all this when there's the chance I'll just have to have another C-section.

Also, I feel shocked by what the whole thing was like. I had had very high standards for my conduct during labor. I have an almost unhealthily high pain threshold, so I assumed this would be a piece of cake. A few years ago, I had an ovarian cyst that ruptured, and I walked into the emergency room. I was so calm about it that they couldn't figure out what the problem was. Apparently, the symptoms for an ovarian cyst are similar to the symptoms for appendicitis, and one test they use to distinguish between the two is how much pain the woman seems to be in. The cyst pain is so extreme that women are in extraordinary distress. And I *was* in extraordinary distress; I just wasn't yelling and screaming.

But in labor, I went totally out of control. I wasn't screaming, but I did swear. Through some of the contractions, I was just going, "Oh shit oh shit oh shit." And there were some contractions where my husband would try to start me on the breathing and I'd just say, "I can't. I can't." And I'd just curl up and moan.

I find that very hard to deal with. The other night, we had some people over, and my husband was telling them about the birth. And he was saying that I was in such awful pain, and "whimpering" and making "animalistic" noises. And it made me really angry. I was thinking, "I was not. I was doing fine. I got through it just fine and then I had to have a C-section." Later that night, we had a fight about it, because I was denying it, and he said, "I didn't make it up; that's what you really sounded like." But I have this need to seem heroic about it.

And then there's something that we joke about a lot now. I'm this perennially *nice* person, and at some point during my hard labor, this very sweet-looking girl who might have been fifteen, a candy striper or something, came in with a breakfast tray and asked if we wanted it. My husband turned to her and said politely, "This really isn't a very good time."

But for some reason, she didn't leave. She just stood there in the doorway with this tray, and so finally I screamed at the top of my lungs, "GET OUT OF HERE!"

I worried about it for days, how I really shouldn't have yelled at her. How maybe I should have let my husband have his breakfast.

t w o

> **Ideal** *"Don't worry, the baby will be fine."*
> **Fact** *Sometimes, the baby isn't the perfect
> infant you dreamed of. And whether the problem
> is a minor infection or a major birth defect,
> coping with the medical treatment and your own
> anxieties can be difficult.*

The books, the movies, and we ourselves assume that the baby's birth will be the climax of the pregnancy drama; after that, we and our perfect newborns will go home and live happily ever after as a family.

But sometimes birth is not the relief we hope it will be. Sometimes, the newborn is whisked away because of unspecified "problems," or trouble develops later in the hospital stay. In the case of a premature birth, the baby will almost certainly need some medical treatment.

Whether the problem turns out to be relatively minor and curable or major and long-term, confronting it can be terrifying. A new life seems terribly fragile whether it is or not, and the uncertainty associated with hospital testing can be hard to bear. You want desperately to nurture and protect your baby, but brisk, white-coated strangers insist they are better qualified to do the job.

The point of this chapter is not to tell you all the things that could go wrong and how to deal with them. But because parents are always so shocked when something does go wrong, you may feel reassured to find some of your own feelings mirrored in the stories that follow.

Old Wives' Tales

A Mysterious Illness Followed by Jaundice

Soon after Sue was born, they discovered that her white blood count was high. They suspected some sort of infection, but they didn't know where it was. So they gave her an antibiotic "just in case" and started doing all these tests to try to determine what was wrong.

I was devastated. You know how your hormones are right after birth. And this was something I just hadn't prepared myself for. It really wasn't that serious, I guess, but when you don't expect it, and then you see your tiny baby with an intravenous feed in her hand and Band-Aids all over her feet because they've pricked her heels a thousand times for blood samples, you just don't feel like you have the emotional stamina to hold on.

When I thought about her getting the tests, I imagined her crying and screaming, and I just couldn't handle it. She wasn't even a day old, and already she had this pain and misery. She seemed so vulnerable, and I was vulnerable with her, because I couldn't help her. I couldn't even tell her that everything was going to be all right, because she couldn't understand. She should have been cuddled and held and nurtured, but instead she was being pulled apart.

Then they told me they had to do a spinal tap, and I got completely hysterical. That sounded to me like a serious medical procedure, and the consequences of it not being administered correctly would be severe. They asked me to sign a form saying I accepted responsibility and they would not be liable. What was I going to say? No? You have to assume that they know what they're doing and that they know more about it than you do. So I just signed it, and hoped it would all work out.

And it did. Actually, they never found out what the cause of the infection was, but the antibiotic seemed to take care of it. So after a few days, we were allowed to leave.

But she was very small and three weeks early, so they wanted to monitor her bilirubin carefully. So the day after we got home, we took her to another hospital for a blood test. They needed to prick her heel again. I couldn't stand it. I sent my husband in with her and just stood outside the door and cried. And after we got home, the doctor called us with the results and said we should take her to a third hospital where they would put her under the lights.

Well, the hospital where I gave birth had been very nice. It was clean, and there seemed to be enough staff to go around, and people were very, very nice to me. And I guess I was expecting that same sort of experience. But this was a much bigger place, and this time she was the patient, not me. The nurses' station was like a zoo, with twenty million people running around and none of them paying any attention at all to us, even though I was standing there with tears streaming down my cheeks. I was so frustrated that no one seemed to be taking care of us, and I was afraid they were going to make me leave her there and go home.

Finally a nurse helped us. She showed us that there was a cot for me to sleep on, although there was nowhere for my husband, so he ended up sleeping on the floor, which was filthy. And remember, this was three days after she was born, and here I was on this flimsy cot, shuffling down endless corridors to get to the bathrooms.

The care was terrible. The nursing staff was stretched way too thin. Every time we wanted to feed her, we were supposed to call and have a nurse find a scale, take her out from under the lights, and weigh her and enter the weight in her chart; and then as soon as she was done, they were supposed to weigh her again and put her back. But it took at least half an hour to get a nurse to come, so eventually we just started doing it all ourselves.

It was heartbreaking to see her under those bright lights, all naked and blindfolded. She had seemed like such a beautiful, healthy child, yet here we were a few days later in a hospital full of seriously ill kids. Luckily, we got out of there in twenty-four hours, and from then on she really was a beautiful, healthy child. But I came down with repeated breast infections, which meant that I was sick and in pain for weeks.

I don't suppose anything could really have prepared me for motherhood except the experience. But I had no idea that it would be such a physical and emotional endurance test.

A Birth Defect with Unknown Consequences
(A Conversation at Three Months)

When Caroline was born, she was completely red, like any baby. But she was a meconium birth, so there were doctors in the room ready to take care of her. After a while, they noticed that a big part of her face was covered by a red birthmark, but they said it was probably the kind of thing that would just fade.

When I was in the recovery room about an hour and a half later, my pediatrician came in and laid out the whole scenario: The mark was a symptom of a vascular disorder, which is usually associated with a whole range of other problems. It is a defect that occurs very early in the embryonic development and may affect parts of the brain, depriving them of oxygen and causing seizures and/or retardation. It can also cause glaucoma, which may or may not be correctable by surgery.

I just wanted to run away. They had no idea yet whether her brain was affected, but they were planning to do a brain scan when she was eight days old. And those were the worst days of my life. My parents came in from out of town, and we all acted as though someone had died. In fact, my father said that even when his mother died he hadn't felt so horrible.

The scan showed that her brain seems normal, but we still don't know what problems might develop down the line. She has already had surgery to correct the glaucoma, and while they were trying to intubate her, they found a blockage in her throat and called in an ear-nose-throat specialist.

So now all we can do is wait to see what happens. The waiting is worse than any of the treatments. But my husband and I feel we've become very intuitive about things, without being flaky or cosmic or religious or anything. We have really good feelings about her eyes and her mental capacity, and he thinks the thing in her throat will just go away.

I've been going to a new-mothers' group, where all the women are supposed to support each other. In the beginning, it seemed good, but I may not be able to continue going. It's hard for me to look at all those little white-faced babies, and the last time one of the mothers seemed to be shunning us, and as I was leaving, I just burst into tears and couldn't stop crying. I'm the only mother who's gone back to work willingly. I went back at six weeks, and, frankly, it was a relief to me to find there was still life beyond Caroline's problems. And I'm the only one who isn't nursing full-time, which makes me feel incredibly guilty.

And, of course, I wonder if the whole thing isn't somehow my fault. The doctors have assured me that it's a chance mutation, that it isn't inherited, and that there's no known external cause.

But I feel much better now than I did two months ago. I would say my postpartum depression was pretty severe. I didn't think I would ever care about life again, about snow or Christmas or working. I guess I realized intellectually that it would just take time to feel better, but that didn't really help.

A Premature Baby

At twenty-two weeks, I had an ultrasound, because my doctor routinely does ultrasounds on women over thirty. Everything went fine. Then, at twenty-four weeks, I started spotting and then really bleeding. I went into the hospital for two weeks, and then it stopped and they sent me home. Two days later, I was bleeding again and in the hospital for another ten days.

They figured out that there was some problem with the placenta, although they weren't sure what it was. Anyway, they wanted to keep me in bed, on my side. I couldn't lie on my back because they said that put pressure on some crucial vessel.

It was such a shock to me because I'd been working a lot of hours and under a lot of pressure, and all of a sudden there I was flat on my back with nothing to do. Mainly, I wanted to keep myself from thinking about it. I just lay there and rubbed my belly and said, "Come on, we'll do this, we'll do this." I'd get myself almost into a trance.

By twenty-eight weeks, they decided I was just bleeding too much and they would have to do a C-section. They offered to take me into the intensive care nursery first so I'd be prepared for what a premature baby would look like and how they might treat it. But I said no. I didn't want to see.

I wasn't conscious for the delivery, and they took her away immediately to intensive care to put her on a ventilator, so I didn't see her. There was no reality to the birth. I remember someone telling me, "You have a daughter," and I cried, but I couldn't really believe it.

I refused to see her for three days. My husband was with her almost all the time, but I wouldn't go. I was very scared. The first three days are the worst in the life of a premature baby. Her lung collapsed. Then she had a hemorrhage in her head, which in premature babies can cause anything from death to blindness to cerebral palsy, which it turns out she does have, although we didn't know it then.

Plus, I was on all these drugs. First they had me on Dilaudid, and when I told them I hated it, they switched me to Demerol. They were giving me drugs to calm me down, and when I told them I didn't want any more, they'd just roll me over and give it to me anyway. I was angry, but I just didn't have the emotional energy to defend myself.

But I was aware of what was happening with her. The doctors were talking to me, and finally they brought me a wheelchair and made me go look at her. It was pretty hard. I don't want to be melodramatic about it, but having a premature child is very confusing. In a normal pregnancy, you have nine months to prepare yourself, and by the eighth or ninth month, you just don't even care if it's going to hurt, you just want to *have* it. I missed those last three months of feeling the baby kicking—and you know, there's a difference between a six-month kick and a nine-month kick.

It was really scary to see her. I didn't feel like she was mine, and, to be honest, I didn't want my baby to be like that. They're so small, and their veins are so tiny they need to have IVs in their belly buttons. They get jaundice. She was fighting the vent, so they had her on a drug to completely immobilize her.

There was really no way to prepare for all the medical procedures we had to go through with her. I felt this amazing affinity for the other moms. I was much more interested in them than in the baby, frankly. I wanted to look at them and talk to them and find out how they were doing. But they were all drugged out, too.

I couldn't hold her because she was hooked up to so many machines. And the atmosphere was tumultuous, with one nurse to every two babies, and lights on twenty-four hours, and buzzers going off. It's like an air traffic control center, and here's this little baby in the middle of it all. And I just didn't want to hold her. The nurses kept telling me, "You've got to touch her. You've got to talk to her." Once I looked at her chart and found they were keeping notes on me: How was I doing? Did I touch her? Did I talk to her? What did I say to her?

It's real hard to feel like she's your child when you have no say in her care. There were times when we were told to leave so they could do some procedure. The first time I really felt close to her was one night, very late, when there was a huge thunderstorm, and I started to think, "What if the electricity goes out? She'll die." And I ran down and asked the nurses. Of course, as they reminded me, hospitals have backup generators.

I was in the hospital for a week after the birth. I had no idea how I was going to cope with anything. When the obstetrician came in to discharge me, I was really upset and I grabbed his hand and said, "Oh, my God, what am I going to do?" And he just disengaged his hand and wrote me out a prescription for Darvon. I'll never forget that. It's other women who got me through, my mother, my sister, other mothers. I never called that doctor again.

She stayed in the hospital for twelve weeks, but I went home after a week. My physical recovery happened very fast, because of course I had no baby at home to nurse and get me up at night. After three weeks or so, I went back to work. The first day was wonderful. It was the first time I'd felt normal in months.

I'd go and visit her before or after work. There wasn't really much I could do except hold her and rock her, and you can only do that for so many hours before they'd take her away to do some procedure or test.

Then one day the hospital called me up at work and told me we could bring her home that night. She came home on a portable apnea monitor, and there was a whole complicated system for keeping track of the machine, plus we had to take classes in CPR. The very first night home, the apnea alarm went off nineteen times, and we ended up taking her back to the hospital the next day.

We were supposed to have a big meeting at work the next day, and I just called up and quit.

I hadn't really given that decision much thought. My intention, if I had had a normal child, was to go back to work full-time. Then, when she was born . . . all I could think about was, was she going to live? Was I going to live? My employers were real nice about it. They said I could come back whenever I could, in whatever capacity I wanted to. But once I brought her home, I realized I couldn't take this baby to a sitter on her monitor. I was pretty sure she was the only baby I was ever going to have, and I thought she deserved to have me.

Also, there's the guilt. You can try to be rational, but there's always this feeling that your body failed you and failed the child. You go over and over everything that might have caused it—was it that aspirin I took, or the Coke I drank? There's just this horrible deep-down feeling of failure and guilt. I've gone through life with few physical problems and without really thinking about a lot of things, but this child I brought into the world isn't going to have the same start. How could I work?

I feel that I have to get her to a point where she can join her peer group confidently. I can't take her to day care till she learns to walk. I can't put her in a group of two- and three-year-olds when she's just learned to sit up. I want her to go into her own world on an equal basis.

Recommended Reading

The Premature Baby Book: A Parents' Guide to Coping and Caring in the First Years by Helen Harrison with Ann Kositsky, R.N. St. Martin's Press, New York, 1983.

three

Ideal *Once you've given birth, your body quickly returns to its pre-pregnant form and function.*

Fact *If you thought recovery was simply about watching your stomach flatten and your bleeding diminish, you may be surprised at the number and complexity of the adjustments your body has to make. And the process may continue well beyond the six-week period traditionally allotted to postpartum recovery.*

A few generations back, a woman giving birth in a hospital would stay there, in bed, for three or four weeks afterwards. Then, during World War II, when London maternity wards frequently needed to be evacuated because of bombing raids, doctors made the discovery that getting women back on their feet quickly actually speeded up the recovery process. And since that time, the typical hospital stay for a normal delivery has been diminishing, from a week or two in our mothers' generation to a day or two in our own.

In addition, there's a more urgent need for a new mother to get back on her feet quickly these days. Few women have enough help, either hired or from family and friends, to allow them a leisurely recovery. And a woman on maternity leave often needs to get back to work after six weeks; some feel pressure to return even sooner.

On top of that, after long months of awkward bulk, shortness of breath, restless sleep, and endless quests for ladies' rooms, most of us eagerly anticipate the ease and energy of normal physical functioning. So it often comes as a shock that what we are for weeks—even months—after giving birth isn't quite "normal."

Sometimes it's hard to tell what "normal" is supposed to be in those long days and nights of new motherhood. Is it "normal" to still be bleeding red when the books say the lochia should be turning brown? Is it "normal" to experience excruciating pain in your breast every time the baby latches on? Is it "normal" to stay inside for two full weeks after the birth, and if so, how come your next-door neighbor went out to dinner five days after she had her baby?

It's important to realize that this is a book and that, like other books, it can't possibly cover the whole range of experiences that lie within a "normal" recovery. If you have serious doubts about any symptom you're experiencing, call your doctor or midwife and let him or her decide. Nothing in this chapter is intended as a substitute for advice your own health-care provider gives you.

However, doctors and midwives have their limitations, too. One fairly common one is neglecting to explain the rationale of certain instructions, such as *why* you shouldn't go outside or climb stairs. Another is not having much time available to spend on talking about what's normal; many doctors simply hand new mothers a list of brusque instructions and emergency symptoms and wave good-bye until the six-week checkup.

In this chapter, an obstetrician and a certified nurse-midwife tell you what to expect from a "normal" postpartum recovery. The obstetrician, Linda Hughey Holt, is the mother of three and the author of two books on women's health. She practices in Skokie, Illinois. The nurse-midwife, Trisha Woollcott, also practices on Chicago's North Shore, and also has three children. They were selected for this book not only on the basis of their excellent credentials but because of their reputation in the community as accessible, realistic, and sympathetic health-care providers.

■ *General Advice.* TW: The main thing I try to get across in the six-week checkup is that there's a *wide range of normal.* I don't know how to prepare people for how hard it really is. I had two kids, and then, almost fifteen years later, I had another, and I still got into thinking that somehow I was going to be able to sit around playing my cello to my baby, with sunlight pouring into my immaculate house. Many women can't believe how great they feel on the second day, and then they crash on the third or fourth.

At first the days seemed very long because I thought my body was so distorted, and I was very upset around the second or third day when I needed a bath desperately and my mother had to bathe me. I couldn't get up out of the tub myself because of the numbness and the weakness in my muscles. That really embarrassed me, because I felt I wanted to be able to take care of myself. But then I was surprised by how fast all those desperate feelings seemed to resolve.

So many people have *unrealistic expectations*, and then reality seems especially hard. I see that very clearly with infertility pa-tients. They've spent years getting pregnant. They finally have the culmination of all those dreams and hopes and all that effort and money—and they're exhausted. And they don't like it very much. And they can't acknowledge it, because everyone's telling them, "Oh, it's so wonderful. Aren't you happy it's finally happened?" And sometimes they get terribly depressed, because they just can't express their negative feelings and can't accept that those feelings are normal.

▪ *Hygiene.*   LHH: All you need to do for both stitches and hem-orrhoids is make sure that whenever you go to the bathroom, you take a little squirt bottle of water and after urinating or defecating, *squirt the perineal area.* That flushes out the bacteria, and the stitches pretty much heal themselves. Typically, you'll keep feel-ing them for two to three weeks, but some women feel them longer.

Other things—sitz baths, Tucks, creams—all those are comfort measures that are fine if they feel good but not necessary for proper healing. If you're feeling overwhelmed and don't get around to doing them, don't worry.

■ *Hemorrhoid and Episiotomy Comfort Measures.*   LHH: *Sitz baths* can be helpful, and you don't need to have the little pan that sits on the toilet; a regular bathtub is fine as long as the water is *no more than four inches deep* during the first week. If you've had a vaginal delivery, you don't want to get dirty water inside you; up to four inches, your uterus will still be above the water level.

TW: You can take the baths either *warm or cold,* whichever feels better; there's no solid scientific rationale for one over the other. Generally speaking, if you're swollen or have hemorrhoids, a cool bath is going to feel better. If you're healing but not swollen, warm might be better. But the main benefit may just be getting to sit in the tub undisturbed for half an hour.

For both the stitches and hemorrhoids, it helps to *keep your stools soft.* Eat foods with fiber, drink lots of fluids, and if you're on an iron supplement, you may want to skip it for a few days until your bowels are regulated. Iron is constipating.

> I had heard so much about how hard it's supposed to be to go to the bathroom after you have a baby, so that was really on my mind. But I didn't have any trouble with it at all. Basically, right after the doctor put my little stitch in, I got up and pooped and took a shower.

For hemorrhoids, you can apply *Tucks or witch hazel.* Keep either in the refrigerator; they'll feel more soothing if cold. If that's not enough, ask your doctor for a prescription for *Anusol or Preparation H with hydrocortisone,* or just buy over-the-counter hydrocortisone .5 percent and put it on two to three times a day.

For episiotomy stitches, it's better to *sit on hard surfaces* than on soft ones (including the donut they may have given you in the hospital), because soft ones will tend to stretch your bottom more. Do thirty to fifty Kegel exercises every time you feed the baby (otherwise, you forget), and when you do sit on soft surfaces, it helps to squeeze your buttocks together as you sit.

While in the hospital, you may have been given combination ice pack/sanitary napkins, which are very soothing but not available on the open market. You can approximate them by *filling Ziploc freezer baggies with crushed ice.*

I would not classify anything related to the birth as a lot of pain. I thought it was the neatest experience in the world. I guess I had ten days of some discomfort afterwards, a little itching or burning. It was maybe four weeks before I felt it was completely healed. I used the ice packs in the hospital, but once I got home I didn't need anything for comfort.

I had a huge episiotomy, and I couldn't believe how hard the recovery was. I couldn't get in and out of bed. I went through dozens of those ice packs they give you in the hospital, and brought lots and lots of them home with me. I took sitz baths and showers and used spray and sat on an inflatable donut. Now it's been three months and I feel completely fine, except that when we have intercourse, the area feels tight and painful and I really need to be relaxed.

▪ *Bleeding.* TW: Two to three weeks of bleeding is typical, but it may continue for longer. As long as the flow seems to be diminishing, don't worry too much about the duration. You may notice an increase when you go home from the hospital, just because getting home involves more exertion than you've probably made in the hospital. Any time you notice an increase in bleeding, it's probably a sign that you're trying to do too much and that you should stay off your feet for a while. Listen to what your body tells you. An occasional blood clot—sometimes as big as a golf ball—is not unusual as long as the bleeding seems otherwise normal.

Call your doctor if: you're soaking a sanitary napkin every hour for four or five hours, or if the blood has a foul, fishy odor and/or your abdomen feels tender, or if you're passing clots with heavy bleeding.

I was wearing a belt and two gigantic sanitary napkins, which were completely unwieldy, and one of them would always turn sideways. I had a whole bunch of blue plastic squares of absorbent material I had to keep putting down on the bed and anywhere else I sat down. Eventually, my husband had the bright idea of going out and buying a package of those undergarments for incontinent old people. That let me get through the night without changing my "diapers."

About two weeks after I had her, I was taking a bath, and all of a sudden I noticed something in the tub that looked like a chicken liver. I screamed and jumped out of the tub and called the doctor. He said not to worry; I must have been bleeding a lot and this was a blood clot. I said, "Are you sure it's not a piece of the placenta?" He said no, a blood clot could be that size. And after he said it was normal, I felt much better. I always thought a blood clot was the size of a pinhead.

I bled for about six weeks after my cesarean, which surprised me. I knew you'd bleed after a vaginal delivery, but somehow I imagined that with a C-section, they'd vacuum you out or something.

- *Common Restrictions.* LHH: It's good to *avoid heavy lifting*— anything heavier than the baby—for a couple of weeks. Then, gradually work your way into some abdominal exercises. The reason I advise this is that the abdominal wall muscles tend to separate during pregnancy, and it's better to let them go back into position naturally than to strain them by lifting things.

I don't restrict people on *stairs*, but I do tell them that climbing stairs may hurt and pull at their stitches. It's a good idea to organize the household so you don't have to run up and down stairs all day.

I don't tell people anything about *going outside*. There aren't any medical reasons not to, although of course if it's bitterly cold, you're not going to want to take the baby. You need to make sure you're getting adequate rest and you don't feel dizzy when you stand up. Most people who are up and around the house and feeling fine can certainly be outside.

For the first week or so, I felt very weak. I first actually walked down some stairs about four days after having the baby, and we walked around outside for about ten minutes and then came back in and that was our big thing for the day. We were shot after that. But I just felt I needed to see the sky.

I stayed in for two weeks, partly because I didn't have a stroller, but also because I just felt very tired. It's been five weeks and I'm still not going out very much, because I get tired pretty easily.

I had a C-section, and a month later I was playing volleyball.

TW: Pay attention to your bleeding and how you feel. If you're bleeding heavily and feel like a wet washrag, you're overdoing it. If you feel fine when you go out, and the next day you also feel fine, then you *are* fine. It's not always a progression from weak to strong; some days you may feel you can do a lot and some days you may not feel like you can do anything. Lack of sleep has a lot to do with it, too, of course.

LHH: With *driving*, the problem is that you may feel groggy or dizzy for several weeks, or if you've had a C-section, it may hurt to lift your foot onto the accelerator or brake pedal. You don't want to get into a situation where you're going to crack up the car because you're not feeling quite with-it. So it's not a bad idea to *wait a few weeks*, see how you're feeling, and when you're up and about and not having dizzy spells and confident that you could react quickly in an emergency, then you can drive.

■ *Cesarean Recovery.* LHH: Most of this advice applies equally to women who've had C-sections and women who've had vaginal births. For C-section recovery, I'd emphasize even more *getting rest* and *no heavy lifting for six weeks.* The stitches don't need any special care, but once a day you should stand in the shower and *let warm water wash over the scar;* don't scrub it, and blot it dry gently.

The scar was less painful than I imagined. It was like a knitting of the flesh, real snug. In the beginning, it was difficult to move in certain ways, and sleeping flat on my back was hard because it felt like the knitting was coming apart. But it only hurt for a few weeks, maybe a month, and not every time I moved.

I was really in excruciating pain afterwards, and they had me on morphine, so I was really out of it the next day. When they made me get out of bed, it felt like all this weight was just slamming down and it was gong to burst right out of the scar. I've never had much experience with pain, so I have nothing to measure it against, but to me it felt really bad.

■ *Breast-feeding.* TW: It's important to know that your *temperature may go up slightly* to 99° or 100°F. if you become engorged when your milk comes in. Don't worry about that, but call your doctor or midwife if it goes to 100.4°F. or above. *Hot cloths* (put wet towels in the microwave, but be careful—they can get *very* hot) or a *hot shower* may make you more comfortable. Be careful to *vary the breast you start with,* keeping track from feeding to feeding by pinning a safety pin to the appropriate bra strap. To avoid or alleviate nipple soreness, *vary the positions* you nurse in. Drink *lots of liquids* and get as much *rest* as you can.

Even if you plan to use *relief bottles* eventually, *don't offer any for the first two to three weeks.* The baby has to suck on a rubber nipple in a different way, and it may confuse her. That starts a cycle where she may refuse the breast, and then you may not be nursing frequently enough to establish an adequate milk supply.

After a few weeks at the breast, most (though not all) babies will go back and forth from breast to bottle, especially if someone other than mom gives the bottle.

If you run into *trouble with nursing*, don't automatically stop. You may be able to solve the problem with help from your doctor, a good book on breast-feeding (see page 95), the La Leche League (see page 95), or your hospital's lactation consultant (call and ask if they have one).

■ *When Breast-Feeding Is Difficult.*   LHH: I try to prepare people to expect breast-feeding to be a *round-the-clock commitment*—to let them know that that's normal. The books all say breast-fed babies nurse every three to four hours, but in reality they may want to nurse every hour and a half or every two hours. That's why you need to have help, because few people can do that every two hours for more than a few days without becoming exhausted. If you're going to be up that much at night, you need to have someone available who can walk the baby around during the day so you can catch up on some of that sleep.

There's no one right solution for any particular problem. For the woman who gets really sore, the answer might be nipple shields, or it might be to have someone else give the baby an occasional bottle. A lot of nursing is about *trial and error*, and asking everyone you know who might know something about it what worked for them.

I try to get everyone to *try breast-feeding*, because I think it has medical advantages for both mother and baby, and I think it's what nature intended. I'm a working mother who has breast-fed two kids, and that helps me a lot in talking to women who automatically decide against it because they think it will be too much work or that they can't go back to work and still nurse.

But I would separate those women from the ones who try and then run into problems. I think it's very important for *those* women to feel very supported in whatever decision they make. This is an era in which women, particularly upper-middle-class women, are under a lot of pressure to breast-feed, and *it may not be for every-*

body. There are a number of perfectly valid medical and psychological reasons why someone should just decide that it's too much, and I'd hate to see someone get started off in motherhood on the wrong foot just because nursing isn't working out. It's only one aspect of motherhood.

A lot of times with this issue, you're in a no-win situation. I remember once sitting at a departmental picnic, out in the middle of a baseball field, when my two-month-old started to get fussy. And I turned to a friend and asked, "Well, should I go ahead and nurse her, and offend all those people who are against nursing in public? Or should I give her a bottle, and offend all those people who think babies shouldn't get bottles?"

(For more on breast-feeding vs. bottle-feeding, see chapter 6.)

▪ *Sex.* TW: The standard guideline on resuming intercourse is to wait *two to three weeks after a vaginal delivery* and *six weeks after a C-section,* unless your doctor tells you a good reason otherwise. But many women aren't too interested at this point. And many women try and find it very uncomfortable.

It's important to remember that a breast-feeding woman is usually hormonally menopausal, with estrogen and progesterone at rock bottom. This means the vagina won't stretch and won't lubricate well. So you want to *go slowly* and use *lots of K-Y Jelly.* I also suggest being on top, which may make you feel more flexible and in control, and also that you can pleasure each other without actual intercourse.

It's been six weeks, and neither of us is in any terrible hurry. It's really a matter of how we want to use our awake-time right now. For sex? No, I think we'll wait.

We waited six weeks, because I had a C-section. But I found it very difficult to wait that long. I was mentally ready a week after the birth. I think it was because having my husband close to me through the whole birthing process made me love him even more.

I had a real different feeling down there, because of the episiotomy. It was painful. Not unbearably, but the skin didn't seem to stretch like it should have. It seemed tighter. I almost cried about it, because I thought it would never be the same, that I would never look forward to it again. But that passed with time.

■ *Weight and Diet.*   LHH: You can probably expect to *lose about fifteen pounds at delivery,* and then *five to ten pounds will come off easily in the first couple of weeks.* Anything beyond that is body fat and is going to need to be dieted off. But it's more important to eat nutritiously and get up and about than to fixate on your weight. For the first six to eight months after the birth, your job is getting adjusted to motherhood and getting adjusted to the baby. You can feel a little depressed about the weight and still recognize that it's not your biggest priority in life right now. You have a long life ahead of you in which to worry about your body image.

TW: *Does breastfeeding help you lose weight?* For some women, it does. For some women, it absolutely doesn't, and they can't lose it until after they wean. Theoretically, it should burn up 500–600 extra calories a day—but there are also the issues of how much you're putting into your mouth and how much is getting absorbed. (There's evidence that absorption increases during pregnancy and nursing.) The number of pounds shouldn't be your focus; you can eat the right number of calories during pregnancy and gain the right amount of weight and still be malnourished and have a malnourished baby because you ate junk. Your focus should be on eating well.

I gained twenty-seven pounds. I was very careful when I was pregnant, and I had her seventeen days early. I lost about twenty right away, and then I lost the rest without really trying within three months. I'm so busy that I hardly have time to eat. I feel like my body looks exactly like it did before I got pregnant, but I remember for the first month I didn't think it ever would. I did sit-ups and went running, and it took a lot of self-discipline because it wasn't anything I really felt like doing.

I gained sixty-five pounds. About thirty to forty came off right away, before the six-week checkup, without trying. But then nothing came off. I stopped nursing at six months because I wanted to get pregnant again, and I noticed that right away my body started changing and I got my waist back. Some people say they lose weight from nursing, but I just couldn't.

The rest of it didn't really come off till I got motivated and started exercising. I would do the Jane Fonda tape in the mornings, while the baby lay on my bed and played with my wallet.

- *Sleep Deprivation.* LHH: The first two weeks, it's normal to feel absolutely terrible and not know which end is up. Most people have never gone through sleep deprivation until they have a baby, and they're completely unprepared for what it does to their system. I went into first-time parenting fairly self-confident about it because I'd been an intern and a resident and I'd been sleep-deprived before. And I can tell you, the worst residency in the world isn't like having a newborn. With a residency, you may be up for thirty-six straight hours, but then you can crash for twelve. With a newborn, it's night after night after night, and that can be devastating.

If you get to the point where you're completely nonfunctional, you should *call your doctor or midwife* and ask about coping techniques. I'll often recommend that *the husband or someone else take over for a night or two,* even with a breast-fed baby, just so the mother can have some uninterrupted sleep.

We've worked out a system where my husband sleeps in the guest room and I sleep in our room with the baby, and we set up the baby monitor so my husband can hear him right away when he wakes up, come get him, change him, hand him to me for feeding, and go back to sleep. That works out well for

When to Call Your Doctor or Midwife

Emergency signs (call any time of the day or night):
- Excessive bleeding (saturating a sanitary napkin every hour for more than four hours)
- Bleeding with foul-smelling, fishy odor
- Temperature of 101°F. or above
- Shaking, chills
- Constant lower abdominal pain
- A vein or area in the leg that feels sore and tender, or having one leg swell up more than the other
- A red, warm area on a sore breast
- Feeling that you may be about to hurt your baby or yourself

Serious signs (call during regular office hours):
- Anxiety, nervousness, depression, and/or sleeplessness that seem to have gotten out of control
- Significant marital problems

me, too, because if I have to get up to change him, then I'm up and I can't go back to sleep.

I still feel like I'm lagging, and the way I deal with it is by not thinking more than about twenty-four hours ahead. I won't make plans to do something with someone next week because how do I know what kind of a rotten night we might have the night before?

I had to go back to the hospital two days after I got out, and one of the nurses took me aside and said, "You look terrible. Are you getting sleep?" And I hadn't. The baby wouldn't sleep, and my breasts were painfully engorged, and I hardly ended up sleeping at all for six to eight weeks. I feel like I aged a lot. My hair even started to turn gray around the temples. I'm sure the depression I had was mostly from being tired. I thought I would never go back to feeling normal, but of course eventually you do.

If I don't get enough sleep and I don't get bathed, I get very strange. I become a monster, and I start thinking I'm a bad mother. I've put a sign up on the door that says, "Mother and Baby Asleep, Please Phone First." But I never answer the phone. I don't even screen calls; I just leave it on low and listen to the whole tape about ten hours later. Or I let my husband deal with it, and take messages.

What I got wasn't so much depression as anxiety. I'd have these strange thoughts, like what if I turned a corner too fast and hit her head against the wall? If she cried for a long time, I'd start thinking about all those people who mistreat their kids, and I'd feel like I started to understand.

■ *Baby Blues and Postpartum Depression.*   LHH: Part of what accounts for the blues is a rapid depletion of estrogen levels. This doesn't affect everyone the same way, but it can cause *hot flashes, depressive symptoms,* and *trouble concentrating.* Usually it resolves itself, but sometimes it's prolonged by breast-feeding, and then the woman and her health-care provider together must decide whether the benefits of nursing outweigh the disadvantages of having the mother estrogen-depleted.

TW: Sometimes women have a very extreme version of what they assume is postpartum baby blues, but it lasts longer. They're *jittery, nervous,* and *can't sleep.* Sometimes it turns out to be a *thyroid imbalance,* which we can check with a simple blood test. Some studies show that 10 percent of postpartum women have some thyroid imbalance. Usually it resolves spontaneously and is rarely treated, but knowing that it's not "all in your head" can be very comforting.

If they still feel the same way a week later, we might send them for *hypnosis* or *relaxation therapy.* Or sometimes we talk to the husbands or families and try to arrange for more support and help at home.

I only stayed in the hospital three days after my C-section. They wanted me to stay longer, but I wanted to go home. It was the stupidest thing I've ever done. I got no rest, and no practical support. There were people who came to "help out" who would come into the bedroom when I went to nap and sit down at the foot of the bed to chat. I got terribly depressed. I just wanted someone to come and take the child and just give me a week alone. And then I would feel guilty for feeling that way.

I got this feeling that both my mother and my mother-in-law had this sort of imagined reality about pregnancy, childbirth, and actually caring for the baby. They were both wonderful mothers, but I don't think they remembered much about the day-to-day reality of it.

Finally, my doctor called my mother to tell her I needed some practical help.

■ *Menstruation.*   LHH: Typically, a women will get her period again after *two to three months if she doesn't nurse* and after *six to eight months if she does nurse.* But there can be huge variations from these ranges—women who are nursing who get their periods back a month after delivery, and nonnursing mothers who take eight months.

■ *Birth Control.*   LHH: You have to use birth control unless you want another baby ten months after your first. Not a year goes by that I don't have someone walk in pregnant three months after her first baby.

I've seen statistics indicating that among women who don't breast-feed, without birth control 90 percent will conceive again within a year of childbirth. Among women who do breast-feed, 40 percent will conceive.

Most women won't ovulate for several months if they're breast-feeding, but the problem with counting on that is that the start of ovulation varies from woman to woman. By the time she gets her period and knows she's definitely fertile again, she'll already have ovulated. So even a breast-feeding woman should use a barrier method of birth control.

I myself make exceptions for infertility patients—for example, someone in her late thirties who took many years to get pregnant. If she's only planning two or maybe three children, I think the downside risk of closely spacing pregnancies is less than the risk of not being able to conceive again. So if those women want to count on breast-feeding to try to space the pregnancies, I think that's perfectly reasonable.

Recommended Reading

The Year After Childbirth: Enjoying Your Body, Your Relationships, and Yourself in Your Baby's First Year by Sheila Kitzinger. Fireside, New York, 1994.

four

Ideal *You might feel a little weepy in the days following the birth, but it's hormonal, and it will pass.*

Fact *You will probably go through more emotional ups and downs than your occasional weepy fits indicate, and for many external, as well as hormonal, reasons.*

E verybody knows that the hormones of the newly minted mother go completely berserk, resulting in irrational tropical-rainstorm fits of weepiness widely referred to as "baby blues," "maternity blues," or "postpartum depression." For years, this has been the pat and socially acceptable explanation for why the new mother doesn't always act the role of the glowing bundle-of-joy recipient, as seen on TV shows and greeting cards.

And, in fact, there's some comfort in this cliché, which keeps us from seriously doubting our sanity even as we sob through cheap-wine commercials or are reduced to incoherence by the thought of writing a thank-you note.

Yet the "hormones, dear" explanation completely overlooks the complexity of forces reshaping a new mother's life, as does the expectation that after a few days, most women will feel completely rational and ready to cope.

In a very profound way, a woman who gives birth to her first baby is not "herself" for a very, very long time afterwards. No matter how much you wanted the baby, no matter how much joy you felt in her arrival, no matter how much household help you have, you still must, at some point, shed the skin of your old individual self and grow a new one with enough room for this small person-who-isn't-quite-an-individual yet. And while the room-making process is full of warmth and wonder, the skin-shedding is usually promoted by abrasive and irritating episodes in which you can't get the sleep you need, don't want sex, have to restrict your mobility, discover you don't have the serenity of a madonna, and perhaps surrender a few of your dreams, at least for the moment.

Of course, the more ambivalent you are about the baby, and the less practical and emotional support you're getting, the harder this skin-shedding is going to be. So that, without actually crying every day or feeling something you'd identify as "depression," you may still find the early weeks and months surprisingly rough going.

Here are some of the most common problems of early motherhood and some suggestions on dealing with them.

■ *Facing Reality.* Pregnancy is certainly a state of mind as well as body; it's not only physically that women are described as "expecting." For nine months you have looked forward to the birth with perhaps mixed amounts of excitement and dread, wondering how labor would go, whether you'd have a boy or a girl, what the baby would look like and act like, and what the effect on your life would be.

You have just come in for a landing.

When you're pregnant, you're always conscious of getting to the end of it. It's like you're running a race. And then, you *do* get to the end. You have the baby. And then you realize that this is actually going to go on and on, for at least eighteen years.

My grandmother is seventy-two years old, and she's just taken her fifty-year-old son back home to care for after a messy divorce. So maybe it never ends.

The first morning I woke up in the hospital, I heard Adam crying in the nursery, and I asked my roommate, "Do you think it's okay for me to pick him up?" She said, "Sure, he's your baby."

When the time came to go home, I was crying so hard. They kept giving me all this equipment: boxes of sugar water, bags of nipples. I thought, "They must be crazy, expecting me to do this by myself." I couldn't believe they were trusting me to take care of him.

I had huge mood swings. On the fifth day home from the hospital, my mother watched the baby, and my husband and I went out to a nearby cafe. Now, my husband is a very energetic person, and he was determined that we were not going to be one of those couples whose life is totally disrupted by a baby. Our life was going to go on as usual. "Oh, we can still have people over to dinner," he said, "and of course we can take him with us to restaurants. . . ."

And I just remember feeling completely exhausted and overwhelmed, and frustrated because there he was, pretending that nothing had changed, when everything had.

■ *The Unrecognizable Body.*   Without giving it much thought, most of us assume that the body we get back after labor will be the body we remember from before pregnancy.

Perception: A madonna-like woman in a diaper ad, dressed in a white gown, sits rocking the baby by an open white-curtained window, bathed in a soft halo of fresh morning sunlight.

Reality: The world's longest and heaviest menstrual period makes wearing white garments inadvisable. Serene nursing makes your contracting uterus cramp. Your hemorrhoids require giant, economy-sized jars of Tucks. Your episiotomy requires constant, undignified dependence on an inflatable plastic donut. Your face may look so exhausted you cannot risk having attention drawn to it with makeup. Your hair seems to have changed texture and suddenly begins falling out. Your breasts are swollen, ache, leak unpredictably and are only precariously contained by large, droopy trap-door bras. Your pear-shaped body may never again know the caress of your favorite blue jeans.

Everyone told me I'd be tired, but I thought that was just because of getting up in the middle of the night. I had no idea my body would need to recover. My bottom was so sore that in the hospital I couldn't move for an entire day. I sat on that rubber donut for two whole weeks. The first time I had a bowel movement, I was so terrified that I had to use my Lamaze breathing.

Sometimes I think that six weeks is a long time to wait to resume sex. Then I think about keeping my bra on so I don't leak all over us, and actually maybe keeping my nightgown on to hide my belly, which is huge and flabby and covered with angry red stretch marks, and of course getting some jelly because I'm so dry, and condoms so I don't get pregnant again. And then I think I'm not in such a hurry after all.

Valentine's Day came about ten days after I had the twins, so I couldn't get out to buy my husband a gift. I decided that my present to him would be to get all dressed up.

So I put on a beautiful silk blouse and all my makeup and went swooshing down the stairs. There he was, with two screaming babies in his lap. He looked up at me and said, "When are you going to feed these babies?"

I burst into tears and said, "Look, honey. This is my Valentine's Day present to you, because I couldn't get out, so I got all dressed up!"

"You look very nice," he said. "But do you think you could please feed these babies?"

■ *Reliving Labor.* As discussed at length in the first chapter, many women find themselves unable to block out thoughts of a labor that seemed to have "gone wrong." If you're blaming yourself for failing some sort of moral or physical labor test, then you may be heading into motherhood at least half-convinced that you're already doing a bad job.

- *Sleep Deprivation.* Unless you've somehow managed to delegate night feeding and comfort to someone else, you're embarking on weeks—maybe months—of lost or interrupted sleep. The result, researchers claim, isn't simply to make you feel more tired during the day. Lack of deep, dreaming sleep will also make you jumpy, intolerant, tense, depressed, and less able to concentrate.

The only cure for sleep deprivation, unfortunately, is sleep. If you can arrange an occasional full night for yourself, you'll be amazed at how much more beautiful the world becomes.

> I was a wreck for at least the first three months. It wasn't just a matter of getting up, feeding her, and going back to sleep. For one thing, after at least one of the middle-of-the-night feedings, she would scream and scream and refuse to go back to sleep and one of us would have to walk her around. I got so tense about it that I couldn't go back to sleep afterwards, even if I was exhausted. I'd just lie awake, waiting for it to start up again.
>
> I've never been able to nap, so I wasn't catching up during the day. And I couldn't work at all, because I couldn't concentrate. When I got into the car, I was an accident waiting to happen.

- *Assuming Responsibility.* The fact that you probably can't arrange a night off (especially if you're nursing and opposed to relief bottles) is one of the biggest shocks to new mothers. It seems logical, somehow, to assume that since we are the mommies and they are the babies, we'll get to tell them what to do. As it turns out, the newborn completely dominates your life.

This may come as a double shock to the woman who regards her marriage as a partnership of equals and therefore assumes her husband will shoulder 50 percent of the responsibility. A number of factors may make this impossible, including nursing (which only you can do), your husband's personality (he may also have trouble adjusting to the restrictions of parenthood), his idea of responsibility (he may feel more pressure to bring home the bacon, especially if you're leaving a job for good), and *your* idea of responsibility (if you *seem* willing to accept it, why shouldn't he let you?). (For more about these issues, see chapter 8.)

I just didn't anticipate the intensity of the responsibility. You can have a dog or a cat or a goldfish and just leave them in the house while you go shopping, and leave them with neighbors while you go on vacation. But you have to be there with a baby all the time, and when the baby cries, you have to know how to respond.

In this job, you're on call twenty-four hours a day and you don't get coffee breaks.

■ *Lack of Control.* The most frightening aspect of this enormous new responsibility is that it lands with a great thud on your shoulders before you have enough experience to feel completely secure about handling it. If you have fed her and burped her and changed her and she still screams herself purple in the face, the only possible conclusions seem to be that (1) something is seriously wrong and you are too incompetent to identify the problem and solve it or (2) the problem cannot be identified or solved. When a helpless infant is so clearly miserable, neither possibility is encouraging.

I was very nervous till he was about six months old. If he had a little rash, I thought it was something horrible. I jumped every time he cried. I was terrified that he would get sick. I ran into his bedroom constantly to check on him. After he'd go down for the night, I'd check on him three or four times in the first hour just to make sure he was still breathing, to make sure he didn't die of crib death.

It's a constant experiment. I'm trying to get her to take the bottle now because I don't want to keep breast-feeding forever. And sometimes she will, and sometimes she won't. I don't know why, and the doctors don't seem to know why, because they tell you all these different things: She won't take it because you just nursed her, or because she doesn't like the kind of nipple you're using. Sometimes she'll throw up after the bottle and I don't know if it's the breast milk or the formula or the combination, or whether the milk was too cold or too hot.

I'm just starting to realize that there may not be answers for everything. But it's hard, because I feel better when I can do something, and I'm never sure whether I've really tried everything there is to try. When she cries, I cry with her. My husband can keep on watching his baseball game and only periodically look over at her and cringe. But I have to keep telling myself that we'll just have to wait this period out.

At the beginning, I thought I'd completely ruined my life. I'd sit up at night trying to think of ways to rectify the problem, because I'm so used to being able to solve problems. But I couldn't think of any way to solve this one. I mean, I couldn't just bring him back to the hospital, or trade him in. I felt really stuck. I thought, "You got yourself into this, and there's no way out."

But as things have settled down into a sort of routine, I've gradually come to feel more normal. I got to feel more comfortable with him, and he really started smiling. Once they smile, it makes an incredible difference.

Eventually, your nervousness will just dwindle away, for a variety of reasons. Babies do less inexplicable crying as they get older. They also become better at communicating their needs, and you become much more sensitive to these needs as you come to know the baby better. You may also find that your need to feel in control of everything begins to diminish under the overwhelming evidence that you simply can't be, and as evidence also accumulates that the baby thrives despite mysterious bouts of fussing.

■ *Domestic Chaos.* How good you feel about life during this period certainly depends in part on your standards for orderly domesticity—and whether you have enough help to maintain them. Tolerance of dust balls, dirty dishes, and frozen food is a clear evolutionary advantage for the new mother.

Unfortunately, whatever practical help you can arrange for now may have a heavy price. If your husband is willing to stay home, he'll probably have to use vacation time. Hired help is expensive and may be intrusive. Relatives can also be intrusive, especially if they stay with you instead of coming for daily visits.

My mother came for a week and drove me completely crazy. I pretty much knew she would, but I let her come anyway because I didn't know how to stop her without hurting her feelings. She worked very hard the whole time, scrubbing the floors, making me feel guilty that she was doing it and worried that she was exhausting herself.

And she offered suggestions about everything. She always thinks her way is the only way, and when we did things differently, she'd either criticize us or get very quiet and withdrawn. Actually, my husband took most of the criticism, because I was just staying in bed and nursing but not doing much of the diapering and comforting. And she'd keep commenting on how much he held her or how much he stimulated her.

We didn't confront her while she was here because we were afraid of hurting her. But on some level she must have realized what she was doing, because the first time I talked to her after she left, she didn't actually apologize, but she kept saying things like, "It's good you're on your own now—you need to find your own ways of doing things."

■ *"Friendly" Advice.* It is not only the pregnant woman but also the brand-new mother who is considered public property. Just as when you were pregnant you unwillingly elicited labor stories from every passing veteran, now you will magnetically attract tips, stories, and "common knowledge" about feeding, sleeping, burping, dressing, diapering, spoiling, and "airing out."

However kindly meant, this advice is almost invariably irritating to receive. Unless it comes from a source you completely trust, its ultimate effect is usually to make you defensive about some policy you've decided on but aren't quite sure yourself is foolproof. And you may resent having to justify yourself constantly.

There are three ways to deal with unsolicited advice: Grit your teeth and ignore it; humor the giver and ignore it; or repel it with Expert Opinion:

There were days when Tom would just scream and scream, and I'd just have to get out of the house. So one day I put him in the carriage and rolled him down the street, screaming, and this old woman came out of a coffee shop and started following us, demanding to know why he didn't have a pacifier in his mouth.

Normally, I try to be nice to little old ladies on the street, but this one was like, *"J'accuse!"* So I said between clenched teeth, "He doesn't like pacifiers," and started walking faster. And she just trotted alongside, saying, "You should *make* him take a pacifier. The way he's screaming like that, flies will go into his mouth!"

He's three months old, and fat and happy on breast milk. But I went to visit my parents about two weeks ago, and everyone went on and on about cereal, so I let him have some. He ate it like a little piglet. But I'm not giving it to him regularly; I just did it to make them feel better.

My mother-in-law talks about it all the time, and I just tell her that I am giving him cereal. He was christened last weekend, and he behaved beautifully, and her comment was, "See how good he is? That cereal is really good for him."

I just tell them what they want to hear and go ahead and do what I want to do. How long are you going to be around them, anyway? A weekend? Then you go home, and he's your baby.

She never came right out and said it, but my mother disapproved of my nursing. You know how the hospital gives you the formula to take home with you? Well, I just wanted to ditch it. But she said, "No, no, take it home. It might come in handy." After she left, I threw it out.

Then she'd say, "People usually give up nursing after two months or so because the babies get too heavy."

So I decided to drown her in information. I went to La Leche League meetings, and I started collecting clippings about how breast-feeding seems to reduce the chances of breast cancer and fights obesity and helps you handle cholesterol later in life. And I put them all into a book where I could refer to them if I needed to.

Then when she said something negative, I started referring to all this information. And that seemed to help her handle it better. She hardly ever brings it up anymore, even though Christine is fifteen months old now and I'm five months pregnant and still nursing.

▪ *Shifting Identity.* Besides making your own emotional adjustments to the fact of motherhood, you may find that your public image is shifting. It began in pregnancy, when you may have felt people were beginning to treat you more as *a pregnancy* than as *you.* Conversations tended to turn to your state (How were you feeling? When was the baby due? Was it planned? Did you want a girl or a boy?).

Once you actually have the baby, the spotlight sweeps past you and onto him or her—with you as spokesperson. And whether you enjoyed the attention or resented it, being relegated to the "mother of" role can be disconcerting. Enormous concern will be expressed about how the baby is eating and sleeping, but perhaps none for how *you* are eating and sleeping.

The other day I was reading something I'd written when I was pregnant about how I felt no one could look beyond my stomach. And it made me think about how, after the baby is born, no one really looks beyond the baby. On the playground, you're known as Tina's mom. Even my parents are now only interested in talking about her. Of course, they come from a time when young parents were absolutely consumed with their babies. When my mother had her children, she was a wife and a mother and that was it. No one expected her to be able to talk about much besides diaper rash.

I find it queer to think back on what I thought about and talked about before childbirth and what I think about and talk about now. Roger comes home from work and talks about work, and I talk about the baby. My friends call and talk about their jobs, and I talk about the baby.

I didn't realize how exhausted I would be three weeks after the birth, but I'm getting back to work anyway. Since I'm just starting my own free-lance business, I'm afraid to say no to prospective clients. And I don't want to give up that side of my life. When my husband comes home at night, I don't want the whole focus of my conversation to be the color of the baby's poop.

- *Isolation.* In ordinary circumstances, most people facing the sorts of challenges you are facing now do so in groups and develop a camaraderie that helps pull them through the stress. When you took your first set of final exams, everyone around you went through it, too. When workers are under business pressures, they are usually surrounded by colleagues under similar stresses. When medical students are confronted with both intense pressure and sleep deprivation, they are surrounded by classmates in the same boat.

New mothers, by contrast, tend to be extraordinarily isolated in a society as mobile as ours. Their everyday friends may be work friends, from whom they tend to withdraw during the postpartum period. Close personal friends may live far away and may be child-less. Friends and relatives who've experienced life with a newborn tend to develop a queer amnesia about its more frustrating aspects. And if your husband leaves for work each day, you may have trouble explaining to him why what you're doing at home all day is extremely exhausting work.

Compounding the problem is the fact that getting out of the house with a newborn may be—or at least may seem—impossible, especially in the winter. And you may have trouble thinking of places to go.

My mother left on Sunday, and on Monday Roger went back to work. I've never really been the kind of person to get depressed, but that was a really hard time for me. Here I was, alone with the baby. And the baby couldn't *do* anything. And he was up all the time. You hear about these babies who sleep all day—not him. He sleeps maybe fifteen minutes at a time and then he's up again. Even when he first came home, he was up for an hour and a half, and then he'd go down for maybe an hour, and then he'd be up for another hour.

That first week after my mom left was really hard. I cried a lot. I'd call my husband at the office, and before he could even ask how I was, I'd be in tears. And he'd say, "Look, I'll get home as early as I can."

It was early December, and I was supposed to be doing Christmas shopping, but I was afraid to take him out. The pediatrician had said not to take him anywhere for four weeks or six weeks. So I was home all the time, and I felt like I was going through withdrawal from society. We just walked around the house all day, looking out the window and into the refrigerator. I called it the Home Tour.

In the beginning, I was afraid to take her out because I didn't know what I would do if she started crying. I felt I could control the situation much more at home. For weeks, I wouldn't go to the supermarket till my husband came home at night and took care of her. What would I do if she started crying in the checkout line? Everyone would turn and look at us and someone would say, "Why can't you control your child?"

But eventually, you get sick of doing the grocery shopping at 8:00 or 9:00 P.M. The first time I finally took her, she started crying on our way out to the car, and I thought, "I just can't do this." But I made myself go ahead, and in the car she stopped. In fact, I think the car calmed her down. In fact, I think the reason she probably started crying in the first place was that she sensed how upset I was about the whole thing. So I just kept taking her out, and gradually I just got more comfortable about it.

■ *Ambivalence about the Baby.* Many women instantly feel a tremendous emotional fulfillment at the birth of their babies, but many do not. And many of those who feel it at birth find their enthusiasm waning as the early weeks at home wear on. Because of their consciousness that something known as "bonding" is supposed to have taken place, they worry that something is wrong with them or that they will never develop a good relationship with the baby.

The day she was born, I felt an immediate attachment. It was overwhelming. I never imagined a love could be so instant, that a relationship could be that gratifying so quickly, especially when it was so one-sided. The birth was a miracle, but I thought my feelings were also a miracle. I kept looking at her and thinking, "I can't believe she's mine."

It wasn't this mystical rush of immediate love. But right after the birth, everyone else was exhausted, and I got this incredible rush of adrenaline. He nursed right off. And then we just stared at each other. And he smelled wonderful. He smelled just like me.

It's been five weeks, and I don't feel bonded yet. I feel about him the way you might feel about a cute puppy or kitten.

Meeting Other Mothers

Meeting other new mothers usually isn't a problem. You automatically have something in common with every single woman who's had a baby within the last year or so, and all of them (yourself included) are fair game for such classic opening lines as, "How old is she?" "How was your labor?" and "Is he sleeping through the night yet?"

The trick is holding onto them once you've done your superficial chatting. Some suggestions:

■ *Be Open.* Being open means starting conversations with new mothers you see on walks or while running errands, and trying to get phone numbers of women who seem nice or live close to you or have a baby your own baby's age. Use your judgment, obviously—but you don't have to absolutely adore someone to follow up. There's a networking among mothers similar to the kind of networking that goes on among office colleagues. With a mother-friend who lives nearby, you can trade tips and, occasionally, an hour of baby-sitting.

■ *Join a Group.* In urban and suburban areas, there are sure to be organized groups of mothers with infants—usually exercise classes or support groups. The exercise classes may be oriented toward you (the baby lies in a carrier or on a blanket and watches you flail around) or the baby (you manipulate the baby's limbs while singing silly songs), but in either case it is mostly a pretext for meeting other mothers. Support groups include general-interest as well as specific-interest groups—for example, mothers recovering from cesarean birth, mothers of multiples, single mothers, mothers of disabled children, and breast-feeding mothers.

To find out what groups exist in your area, try calling your childbirth education teacher, your doctor or midwife, the hos-

pital where you gave birth, and community and church organizations. Many cities and regional areas have free monthly
parenting publications that list local resources and activities.
Look for them in maternity stores and shops that sell children's
products, including book, toy, and furniture stores.

- *Form a Group.* If the group you want to join doesn't exist,
found it. A talk group requires only a room full of chairs or
pillows. You could start an exercise class with a large room, a
VCR, and an exercise tape. To start a special-interest group,
you might see if you can contact an existing organization in
another area and find out how it's run. Advertise in the newspaper or on bulletin boards to find other interested mothers.

I had read about bonding, and I'd hoped to bond with
her immediately. But in the beginning, I just felt fond of her,
not this deep, overwhelming love. It wasn't till after at least
two weeks, when my mother had left and my husband had
gone back to work and I was left completely alone with her,
that I really began to feel deeply.

Still, I've felt anger and resentment toward her because
she keeps me from doing work I want to do. When she falls
asleep, I run to the computer to work on my dissertation, and
sometimes she wakes up sooner than I think she should, and
I feel very frustrated and anxious. And maybe she senses
that, because it always seems to make her fussier.

- *Breaking Up with the Doctor/Midwife.* Even if you didn't seem
to have a terribly personal relationship with your doctor or midwife, you may find saying good-bye at the final postpartum visit
surprisingly difficult. For months now, he or she has been the one
person who not only expressed regular interest in your progress
but was willing to claim some responsibility for it. To be cut loose
now, at a time when (for all the above reasons) you may not feel
terribly sure of yourself, can be scary, and a little like pulling the

Postpartum Panic: Where to Get Help Fast

One of the biggest challenges of new motherhood is finding the help and support you need when you need it. Over the long haul, family and friends are extremely important to the happiness of your everyday life. But in the early days, especially if your family is far away or unsupportive and you haven't yet established friendships with other mothers, you may need emergency help for one of the following reasons:

- *The Baby Is Sick.* Obviously, you need medical help immediately if you suspect that your baby is seriously ill. That means calling your pediatrician or family doctor during the day and calling the doctor or your hospital's emergency room at night.

- *The Baby Is Crying Enough to Worry You, but You Doubt that He or She Is Actually Sick.* During the day, call your doctor and ask. In the middle of the night, call the maternity floor of the hospital where you gave birth; the nurses will probably remember you, but even if they don't, they're up all night anyway and can give you advice or reassurance.

- *You Cannot Get Enough Rest.* Ideally, you'll have family or friends helping out with the household chores in the first week or two, and you'll lower your standards of order and cleanliness for a few weeks or months. If that doesn't work out, and you belong to a religious community, your congregation may be able to send volunteers to help out. Otherwise, you might consider hiring help. In most urban and suburban areas, there are agencies that supply daily help on short notice. Look in the yellow pages for an agency specializing in new-mother care; the staff will be trained in dealing with babies as well as doing household work. (You should, of course, ask whether this is the case; also ask for the names and numbers of people who've used the service whom you can call as references.)

- *You Just Can't Cope.* Most new mothers feel overwhelmed at various points in the first weeks or months. There is no clear dividing line between such "normal," transient feelings and what doctors recognize as "serious" postpartum depression. If you feel that you might be capable of harming yourself or your baby, call your obstetrician immediately and ask for help. Unfortunately, not all doctors are sensitive to lesser emergencies, and if what you really need is to talk to someone about what's happening to you, you may not find an eager listener in your obstetrician. Your hospital or childbirth education teacher should have a list of community resources for parents, which might include stress hotlines and new-mother support groups. The hospital may also be able to refer you to a therapist who specializes in women's or family issues.

curtain on the Wizard of Oz: Perhaps you were in charge all along, after all.

When I went in for my six-week postpartum checkup, I got really upset. I was crying like an idiot. I was really embarrassed, but the obstetrician said that it happens all the time.

What Is Bonding?

What is bonding? When is it supposed to take place? Is something wrong with you if you don't fall head over heels in love with the baby immediately after birth?

Bonding, first of all, is not some kind of Apgar-like measurement of your capacity for mother-love administered during the first five minutes of motherhood. It is a theory devised by scientists to explain the way some animals—baby geese, for example—imprint on the first animal they meet after birth. Though human infants are clearly more complicated than baby geese, researchers have wondered whether some equivalent process may be at work in the early hours and days of the baby's life. If so, the routine hospital practice of separating mothers and babies after delivery might have long-term consequences.

"Naturalists" argue that bonding has been another casualty of the medicalization of childbirth—that women routinely bonded with their babies immediately after birth until hospitals began denying them the opportunity. But in fact, as Ann Dally points out in *Inventing Motherhood,* modern medicine may actually have created our modern expectation of an immediately close mother-baby relationship by insuring for the first time that the vast majority of babies born would survive. Some sources indicate that in the eighteenth century, for example, only one out of four infants survived until his first birthday, and that a third of all infants may have died within two weeks of birth. Under those circumstances, mothers were more likely to harden their hearts to harsh reality than invest them in "bonding."

The results of recent bonding research are still highly controversial. Andrea Boroff Eagan, who reviews the evidence quite sensibly and readably in a chapter of her book *The Newborn Mother,* points out that "it does, after all, seem logical that two people will form a stronger attachment if they are together than they will if they are separated, especially if they have barely met and one of them can't talk."

However, Eagan argues, the exhilaration and love some women feel in the delivery room usually do not persist through the early weeks, especially when the woman is lonely and exhausted and the baby cries a lot. The development of social smiling sometime in the second month usually dramatically increases a mother's sense of attachment for her baby. But the relationship may take even longer to jell if the baby is especially demanding or cranky or if the mother hasn't got a solid support system to help her cope.

I went through my whole six-week checkup with a huge lump in my throat. I'm not sure why, exactly. For one thing, I hated being pregnant and I had a horrible labor, so you'd think I'd be relieved that the whole childbirth process was over. For another thing, I didn't really like the obstetrician, and he left for a vacation the morning I went into labor, so he wasn't even the one who ended up delivering my baby.

Still, I had this deep, sad feeling—the way I felt when I graduated from college: like an era in my life had passed forever, and I could never be that young again.

I made it through the examination, but once I got out to the car, I just put my head down on the steering wheel and sobbed.

Recommended Reading

Mother-Infant Bonding: A Scientific Fiction by Diane E. Eyer. Yale University Press, New Haven, 1992.

The Newborn Mother: Stages of Her Growth by Andrea Boroff Eagan. Henry Holt and Company, New York, 1985

This Isn't What I Expected: Recognizing and Recovering From Depression and Anxiety After Childbirth by Karen R. Kleiman, M.S.W, and Valerie D. Raskin, M.D. Bantam, New York, 1994.

five

Ideal *Everything you need to know about raising children is in some child-care book, somewhere.*

Fact *Mothering is about learning to trust your own instincts, regardless of what Spock, Brazelton, Leach, and others have to say on the subject.*

Welcome to motherhood. Once upon a time, it was regarded as an instinctive sort of undertaking. And if women didn't actually have little burping-and-diapering programs written into their DNA, it is true that for most of human history they absorbed everything they needed to know from their own mothers and sisters and aunts, whose own knowledge had been handed down through the centuries without much innovation. In those days, it was clear who the child-care experts were.

Today, judging from the material that gets published on the subject, motherhood is one of the more controversial occupations. Notions about the care and feeding of babies change like hemlines, and the advice our mothers pass down to us is likely to be outmoded. At any rate, we must constantly measure it against the advice doled out by the experts who write books and appear on *The Today Show*. And even if those experts happen to be men who learned everything they know about kids in schools, scholarly journals, clinical studies, and fifteen-minute office visits, they have an irresistible aura of authority simply because they are—well—*experts*.

This is a phenomenon well worth contemplating before you begin your desperate—and probably inevitable—plunge into the child-care literature. How much, really, do the experts know?

Let's say, for example, that your newborn has come home from the hospital happily sucking a pacifier supplied by the nurses. You give it no thought until your neighbor, who's had two babies, remarks that *she* never believed in plugging up her babies' mouths with rubber.

This makes you feel suddenly guilty and a little nervous, so you furtively consult the copy of Dr. Spock your mother gave you. If used "right," Spock advises, pacifiers can be an efficient way to prevent thumb sucking. Of course, he adds, neither activity is really desirable, but thumb suckers tend to cling to their behavior until three, four, or even five years of age, while pacifier suckers can generally kick the habit at three to four months.

You feel vindicated, but also still a little nervous. Now you recognize that the pacifier is forming a habit which will need to be broken. At three months, you are even more nervous; the baby shows no sign of being ready to give the pacifier up. Now you consult Dr. Hugh Jolly's *Book of Child Care*, which one of your aunts brought over. Jolly, you discover, used to be against pacifiers on the grounds that they were unhygienic, but he has changed his mind; now he opposes them because they prevent the baby from sucking his thumb, thus *denying him the opportunity to learn* about his mouth by exploring it with his finger.

Thumb sucking, a learning experience? And if it is, might you already have educationally stunted your baby? You want to check it out. So you go off to the library and take out a whole stack of child-care books and see what other experts have to say on the subject.

T. Berry Brazelton (*Infants and Mothers*, revised edition, 1983): A mother who uses a pacifier *is* just trying to "plug" her baby up. She's using it to control him at her own convenience. Were she to let him suck his fingers, he would learn to comfort himself when he needs it, and thus learn mastery of his environment.

Penelope Leach (*The Child Care Encyclopedia,* 1984): Leach doesn't mention pacifiers, but does approve of thumb sucking, like Brazelton, because of the control it gives the baby. Sucking her fingers, Leach advises, will enable the baby to be confident, to tolerate being spoken to by strangers, and to be left alone in her room at bedtime.

By now, you've probably resolved not to be one of those manipulative parents who stunts her baby's intellectual and emotional development with a disgusting rubber plug. And just as you've decided this, you run across the following passage in Dr. Marianne Neifert's *Dr. Mom* (1986): "It always saddens me to hear a new parent exclaim, 'No baby of mine is going to have a plug in her mouth.' The fear of having a four-year-old with a plug is simply not reason enough to deny a pacifier to a newborn, and only a rare baby will hang onto this behavior until a late age, anyway."

Now, you're right back where you started, except that you could throw some expert citations at your neighbor to "prove" it was okay to let your baby have that pacifier. So you're *right*, but you're a little less confident, because it's now possible that your baby is intellectually and emotionally stunted, sucking an unhygienic toy, and addicted to a habit you may never be able to break.

Putting the Experts in Perspective

Does this mean you shouldn't consult child-care books, that all experts are really quacks? Not at all. In the first place, unless your mother lives with you, you probably don't have someone around to ask questions of all the time, particularly questions about the symptoms of various illnesses—a subject on which Spock, Jolly, Leach, and Neifert have extensive, useful sections.

But it's important to separate that kind of medical advice from all the rest of the advice the books offer. In the beginning, you'll assume there are right and wrong answers to questions like, "Why is the baby crying?" "Where should the baby sleep?" "Can I spoil him by holding him too much?" and "Is it okay to nurse/rock her to sleep or should I just put her down and let her cry?"

Because most child-care books will address such subjects authoritatively, you'll assume the writers have mounds of scientific evidence that back their claims in the same way laws of physics back rocket flights into space. In fact, science these days is more help with making babies than with raising them, and most expert advice reflects the culture, education, era, philosophy, prejudice, and experience (or lack thereof) of the individual who gives it.

One way of making this clear is to run quickly over the ways in which beliefs about child care have changed over the course of the past two hundred years. The following historical crash course comes mostly from the book *Dream Babies*, whose author, Christina Hardyment, believes that "The history of child-care books is no substitute for a modern book of baby-care—but it is an essential antidote." (The chronological divisions and the names for each era are Hardyment's.)

The Age of Nature and Reason, 1750–1820

Survival was the basic child-care issue. An essay written by a British physician in 1765 claimed that 60 percent of baptized children died before they were two years old. Since there were few doctors and consulting one was expensive, a child-care manual would contain the only medical advice a mother was likely to get.

These manuals, the ancestors of our modern ones, tended to be written by doctors who worked in foundling hospitals, and were intended for the nurses. This explains the emphasis such books have placed ever since on regular feeding schedules of three- and four-hour intervals, which were essential to institutional routine but which the doctors also apparently assumed were essential to the babies. (In the twentieth century, John Bowlby's observations on the psychology of children in foundling hospitals would also be assumed to apply to children in general, leading to widespread concern about the effects of "maternal deprivation." See chapter 10.)

Feeding was directly related to survival, yet the advice given may have done more harm than good. Writers gave elaborate recipes for starch-based milk substitutes, babies were not fed vegetables and fruits, and it is possible that the large number of deaths attributed to teething were actually caused by scurvy, a deficiency of vitamin C. It was fashionable to send babies to wet nurses rather than breast-feed them oneself, but great care had to be taken in selecting the nurse, since it was believed that the child drank in characteristics of her personality along with the milk.

Philosophy was an important aspect of child care. While the Puritans still took their instructions from God (a crying child might need to have the Devil whipped out of him), enlightened European parents were profoundly influenced by the writings of John Locke and Jean-Jacques Rousseau. These philosophers regarded children as young savages, from whom adults were removed only by their faculty of reason. Neither had much experience backing his words: Locke had no children of his own; Rousseau had been abandoned by his parents and in turn abandoned his own five illegitimate children to a foundling hospital.

Mothers in Command, 1820–1870

Mothers came to be regarded as the rightful custodians of their children's upbringing as more and more husbands left the house each day to earn family income. As doctors came to know more about physiology, it became clear that strong bodies could be shaped; a parallel "science" of phrenology, which related bumps on the head to aspects of character, encouraged the notion that character, too, could be shaped—intensifying the importance of decisions the mother made.

Breast-feeding by the mother seemed almost to be assumed by child-care manuals of this period, but the experts were full of complicated instructions about schedules and intimidating warnings to nursing mothers to avoid "excessive activity" or "violent passions or emotions," since milk formed under these influences could give the baby convulsions.

Sleeping hadn't seemed an issue to the child-care experts until now, probably because it was assumed that the infant was sleeping with the nurse or the mother. Now writers began to warn mothers to teach their babies to sleep alone from the very beginning, lest they develop habits that would be impossible to break.

Crying became controversial. Some experts believed it signified discomfort or need, while others believed it was nature's way of stimulating infants. Samuel Smiles argued the latter case because otherwise "it would be an anomaly in the benevolent working plan of creation and an unmerited infliction of pain on the little innocents." (A century later, Grantly Dick-Read would use essentially the same argument to deny that pain could be inherent in the childbirth process.)

Cold baths must have been a necessity in most homes, since there was as yet no plumbing. Yet the child-care manuals prescribed them as a means of developing character, and parents were advised to sing loudly to drown out the baby's screams.

The baby carriage was invented, along with a host of other devices designed to keep the baby happy when not being held by a human. Hot debates ensued over subjects including whether the bouncing and jolting of a carriage ride could damage the baby, and in what circumstances one might or might not be seen pushing one's own carriage (as opposed to having the nurse push it).

Schools were founded to care for the preschool (aged two to seven) children of the working poor. Many experts, however, warned middle- and upper-class mothers that a superior moral and intellectual education for children of this age could only be provided at home, by the mother—foreshadowing the day-care debates of our own time.

Science and Sensibility, 1870–1920

Feminism enjoyed a brief vogue in the 1870s and 1880s, encouraging women to worry about their own development rather than their children's. Breast-feeding fell back out of style, and nannies had their Golden Age. This may account for a relative lack of child-care literature published in these decades, as well as a backlash in the decades to follow, when motherhood became a sort of sacred calling, but one for which women clearly needed training.

"Child Study Societies" were formed throughout England and America to collect "scientific" data about normal children. The societies encouraged mothers to record the significant milestones of their children's lives and turn the records in for analysis. From these records came the first widely accepted norms of height, weight, and developmental achievement for various ages—as well as the dawn of the age in which a mother with a baby who didn't fit the norms could really start to worry about it.

Bottle-feeding was all the rage as "scientifically" created formulas based on cow's milk became widely available. The experts offered lots of advice on how feedings should be scheduled (with enough time for the baby's stomach to "rest"), and began to debate the issue of whether or not a baby needed to be held while the bottle was administered.

Bathing in cold water was passé, but Americans were told the ideal temperature for a baby's bath was 80° to 90°F., while British mothers were advised to warm their water to 90° to 98°F.

Sleep suddenly became a training ground for all babies who didn't fall neatly within the strict "norms" now recognized by the experts. Writers assumed that when a baby didn't sleep as much as they insisted he should, it must be a case of insufficient discipline on the parents' part; deprived of this "normal" quota of sleep, parents were warned, their children could develop damage to their nervous systems.

Potty training was a major issue at a time when washing appliances weren't yet available and servants were disappearing. Mothers were advised that training should begin at birth, with laxatives administered to encourage bowel regularity.

Masturbation, thumb sucking, nail biting, nose picking, and *dirt eating* began to appear in the child-care literature as practices that needed to be nipped in the bud. Since it's doubtful that the practices themselves were new, their treatment by the experts underscores how the authorities were beginning to wrest larger hunks of child-rearing turf away from mothers.

Holding or *carrying* infants now came to be regarded as a harmful practice which "cramps their heads and bodies, stops the free circulation of their blood, and often makes them weak in standing." Playpens became popular.

Kissing babies was discouraged, since germs could be transmitted.

Growing Superior Children, 1920–1946

Behaviorism, a school of psychology based on experiments in training animals with rewards and punishments, was the dominant belief among child-care experts, particularly John B. Watson and Truby King.

Watson, whose *Psychological Care of the Infant and Child* (1928) sold more than 100,000 copies, believed the baby's only inborn instincts were fear of sudden noises and of falling, and of rage at being prevented from moving his limbs. Therefore, mothers were responsible for instilling all other characteristics, which they did by conditioning. Since children would have to learn to survive in a tough world, they needed to be hardened quickly; demonstrations of affection were to be avoided at all costs (rather than kissing their children in the morning, parents were advised to shake their hands), and mothers should stay away from their children for as much of the day as possible, letting nannies—who wouldn't be emotionally involved—perform everyday care.

Watson believed a child who'd been overindulged could be identified because he would drop whatever he'd been doing if his mother came into a room and would insist on being cuddled. Ironically, in recent research that purports to assess the emotional stability of children in day-care, such intense attachment to the mother is regarded as the primary indication of "normality."

Truby King, another behaviorist, was an advocate of breastfeeding, but believed the scheduling of the feeds was crucial. All infants must be trained from birth to feed at four-hour intervals during the daytime and to go for eight hours without a feeding at night. Mothers who blanched at listening to their infants scream for hours on end simply lacked willpower; if men could breastfeed, King wrote, they'd certainly be capable of sticking to schedules.

Sleep was becoming a bigger issue, presumably because servants were disappearing and it was now the mother who had to do all the getting up. She was still warned to keep the baby in his own bed, but perhaps the bed could be moved into the mother's room to minimize her disturbance when she did get up. This advice did not apply to Truby King babies, who were just to be left to cry.

"*Crying it out*" became a catchphrase, something the mother let the baby do for his own good. You could tell a crying baby was just being "bad" if it stopped crying once you picked it up; this meant it didn't really need anything but was trying to manipulate you. It was important for most babies to cry, because otherwise they wouldn't exercise their lungs and might get pneumonia.

Fresh air became an obsession. It was part of Truby King's prescription, but he came from New Zealand, where the climate was considerably milder than in England and America. Nevertheless, mothers on both sides of the Atlantic began to believe it was ideal to keep the baby outside for nine to fifteen hours every day. Residents of high-rise buildings were advised to hire a carpenter to construct a special cage outside a window, in which the baby could be left to "air out."

Mouth breathing was another potential disaster which, mothers were instructed, could lead to "ear disease, glandular swellings, and retarded physical and mental development." It was important to check the baby nightly to make sure the mouth remained closed. Also, bad habits like thumb sucking, nail biting, and toe sucking (yes, *toe sucking*) also had to be prevented, because they might result in mouth breathing.

Montessori schools promoted the concept that the proper intellectual stimulation could make children aged two to five smarter and more independent than their parents had thought possible. Meanwhile, the development of intelligence testing produced intellectual "norms" to which children could be compared, another milestone in the evolution of anxious parents. Also, mothers were less and less likely to have domestic help, and children were less likely to have large groups of siblings to play with, two trends which may have accelerated the rush to earlier schooling.

Baby Rules, Okay? 1946–

The current era of baby-care thought is dominated by the work of two men: Sigmund Freud on emotional issues and Jean Piaget on intellectual ones. It was Freud's theories about the consequences of childhood traumas that paved the way for John Bowlby (see chapter 10) and others to argue that anything less than constant contact with the mother could result in something ominously known as "maternal deprivation." Until the second half of the twentieth century, however, most child-care manuals assumed that some, if not most, of a baby's day-to-day care would be handled by servants.

Piaget's contribution was to classify the ages at which babies could be expected to reach various developmental milestones and perform various tasks. From then on, many manuals would be organized chronologically in terms of cognitive development, and writers would suggest that stimulating babies to achieve successive milestones more quickly was an important goal of good mothering.

Between the two of them, Freud and Piaget have fathered the conviction that being away from your baby for any but the most minor absence is bound to damage her emotionally or intellectually, if not both.

Sleeping is now a confusing issue, because the old notion that babies should be trained by "crying it out" hasn't died, but is directly contradicted by a newer, Freudian notion that crying signifies a deep psychological need that had better be met *or else.* Many experts recommend a combination approach in which the baby cries but you go in to "reassure" him with a pat on the back every five or ten minutes. A whole movement of parents questions the premise of barring the baby from the comfort of the mother's bed in the first place.

Crying is no longer attributed to the need for exercise. A newer, Piagetian interpretation is that babies who are full and comfortably dressed may cry from insufficient intellectual stimulation, i.e., boredom.

Carriages are still around, but because they leave babies alone and unstimulated, many child-care writers advise use of front- and backpacks, which promote contact between mother and baby.

Breast-feeding was dangerous territory for strict Freudians because of all the potential for trauma it involved, including weaning and preventing the baby from biting the nipple. At any rate, it remained out of favor in America until its resurrection in the 1970s as part of the holistic and women's health movements.

Currently, breast milk is recognized as the best choice nutritionally, and breast-feeding is advocated by psychologists because it
promotes all the closeness, cuddling, and "bonding" the behav-
iorists disdained so.

Toilet training is a volatile issue; Spock himself has switched
gears three times since 1945, when he advocated leaving the
timing up to the baby. In the late 1960s edition of *Baby and Child
Care*, he advised parents to begin firmly at eighteen months, even
if the child showed no sign of being ready. Then, in the 1970s
edition, he noted that a child could take his time, up to the age
of three.

So What Should You Do?

None of this is meant as an exposé of the child-care book
industry. While publishers make a lot of money publishing these
books, clearly new parents desperately *want* the advice and have
to get it from somewhere.

The secret to getting the most out of child-care books (as well
as from your pediatrician, your mother, and your friends) is this:
*Take only the advice that sounds reasonable to you, and only use it as
long as it works.* If something you read makes you feel guilty or
inadequate, try not to cave in to the feeling; consider the possibility that the writer is simply wrong. Perhaps babies can't be
taught to sleep at night; perhaps they can't be rushed to read
before they're two; perhaps the children of the expert you're consulting grew up and joined a religious cult and never called home
again.

The last word goes to one mother who had two children ten
years apart and took them both to the same pediatrician:

In those ten years, so much about child rearing had changed
that all of his advice was completely different. For instance,

when the older one was two months old, he told me to start her on cereal, and when I said I didn't think she was ready, he said, "She *needs* cereal now."

Then I brought the second one in when he was four months old and mentioned that I intended to start him on cereal. "Absolutely no solid foods until six months!" he thundered.

Recommended Reading

On the history of child care:

Dream Babies: Three Centuries of Good Advice on Child Care by Christina Hardyment. Harper & Row, New York, 1983.

Medical and child-care advice:

Baby and Child Care by Benjamin Spock, M.D., and Michael B. Rothenberg, M.D. Pocket Books, New York, 1985.

Dr. Mom: A Guide to Baby and Child Care by Marianne Neifert, M.D., with Anne Price and Nancy Dana. New American Library, New York, 1986.

What to Expect the First Year by Arlene Eisenberg, Heidi E. Murkoff, and Sandee E. Hathaway, B.S.N. Workman, New York, 1989.

Developmental information and advice:

The First Twelve Months of Life: Your Baby's Growth Month by Month by Frank Caplan. Bantam Books, New York, 1978.

Infants and Mothers: Differences in Development by T. Berry Brazelton, M.D. Dell, New York, 1969.

Practical tips:

Babysense: A Practical and Supportive Guide to Baby Care by Frances Wells Burck. St. Martin's Press, New York, 1979.

Ideal *Nursing is the best possible choice for feeding your baby.*

Fact *While experts almost universally promote breast-feeding, it may not work out for you.*

To nurse, or not to nurse? That question, as the previous chapter demonstrates, is at least as old as child-care literature. A child at the breast symbolizes everything beautiful and tender about the mother-infant relationship. But it has also symbolized—to women throughout history who've had other things besides motherhood on their minds—the way in which a mother is effectively bound to the child for months after the umbilical cord is cut.

Alternatives to nursing have always been available to those women who could afford them. So for women of the upper classes, the decision whether or not to breast-feed has often been dictated by the prevailing notions of what an ideal mother should be. In one era it might have seemed important for a woman to prove that her body continued to be for her husband's pleasure, rather than her child's sustenance; in another era the hygienic risks of wet-nursing or artificial milk substitutes might have made breast-feeding seem the only safe course. In our mothers' generation the smart, modern thing to do was to rely on "scientifically" constituted formulas, which were said to eliminate the mess and bother of nursing.

In our own time the pendulum has swung back, and experts almost universally advise that breast milk is the most perfectly designed infant food, and that it passes on antibodies which help the baby's resistance to infections. Now, women who worry about giving their babies the "best" possible start will, as a matter of course, nurse them.

The trend back toward nursing, however, coincides with another, apparently contradictory, trend: that of mothers returning to full-time work within a few weeks or months of their baby's birth. The two trends aren't *absolutely* contradictory. Many women have discovered that they can work full-time and express and store milk for the baby to drink while they're away. In fact, they say, continuing to nurse takes on an increased significance, since it allows them to continue giving of themselves as mothers at times when they can't be physically with the baby.

Yet in the passion of promoting nursing, many advocates have surrounded the practice with a sort of moral halo, implying that it is what mothers who *really care* about their babies will do for them, regardless of how physically difficult it is or how it fits into the logistics of a working mother's daily life. The idea that breast milk is "nutritionally superior" to formula stirs up a vague image of whole-grain bread versus sour-cream-flavored potato chips, even though it isn't clear that any formula-fed babies have suffered over the long term. The idea that nursing promotes "bonding," included in every exhortation to breast-feed, seems to imply that a bottle-fed infant will grow up slightly alienated and deprived, no matter how much you think you love her. The idea that nursing is "natural" makes every woman whose nipples scream STOP feel (like the woman who can't manage "natural" or vaginal birth) as though she has failed.

The point of this chapter is that nursing is not a moral battlefield in which the good mothers are separated from the slightly insufficient ones. If nursing isn't the best thing for *you*, it can't make you a good mother.

Assuming that you're trying it, or thinking about trying it, or thinking about stopping it, here are a few of the factors that may influence your happiness.

▪ *Physical Factors.* Medical texts currently maintain that there are few physical reasons why a woman wouldn't be able to nurse (use of certain drugs, for example, or repositioning of the nipple during cosmetic surgery. If you have doubts, ask a doctor you trust). But there is no doubt that ease of nursing varies from woman to woman. Inverted nipples may make it harder, though not impossible. Clogged ducts and breast infections may make it extremely painful, although they can be treated. And some women do encounter difficulties with engorgement or undersupply, although these usually indicate a problem with the technique or frequency of feeding rather than with the woman's natural capacity.

You're more likely to have any of these problems right off the bat, and since a newborn needs feeding almost constantly (or so it seems), nursing may make you feel miserable in the very beginning. At this point, hospital nurses, relatives, and friends may start encouraging you to bottle-feed.

One alternative is to do just that, and consider yourself lucky to live in an age of formula. Remember that a whole generation of American babies grew up fine on it, and don't waste time wondering whether you missed a deeply satisfying experience. Other women may find it deeply satisfying, but they aren't in extreme pain while doing it.

The other alternative is to persist and see if the experience improves with time. In order to do this, you desperately need to seek out sources of support for and information about breast-feeding. These *might* include your pediatrician, but if he or she isn't helpful, just keep looking elsewhere. Any individual nurse who helped you while you were in the hospital may be able to give you good advice on a problem that's developed since then. Call the maternity ward and ask for her, or if you can't remember any names, you might just phone the nurses' station and try your luck talking to anyone who happens to be available. You might also ask if the hospital employs or knows of a lactation expert—a nurse who specializes in breast-feeding concerns.

Women who are strongly committed to breast-feeding might consider contacting the La Leche League International, which was founded in 1956 to provide information and encouragement to nursing mothers. The League has chapters in many communities, and these chapters hold regular informal meetings in members' homes. It has also published a book called *The Womanly Art of Breast-feeding*, which you can find in a library or through a bookstore.

It helps to be forewarned that the La Leche League promotes an extremely traditional view of the roles of mothers and fathers in the family. Mothers stay home with children and fathers are expected to provide for and protect them. So if that's not your cup of tea, or if you are trying to integrate nursing with working outside the home, don't look for any support here. If you are interested in attending a meeting, check for notices in your community newspaper, ask your childbirth education teacher if she knows the name of a local leader, or call or write the League headquarters at 1400 N. Meacham Road, P.O. Box 4079, Schaumburg, IL 60168-4079; (847) 519-7730 or 1-800-LALECHE.

Two other excellent books that may help you with the mechanics of nursing—including nursing and working—are *The Complete Book of Breastfeeding*, by Marvin S. Eiger, M.D., and Sally Wendkos Olds and *The Nursing Mother's Companion*, by Kathleen Huggins.

I had trouble with breast-feeding right from the start. I have this growth on one of my breasts that's been there for years but got much bigger in pregnancy. The doctor said it's not health-threatening for me, but when I tried to nurse, it really kept the baby from being able to latch on properly.

He cried all the time; I guess because he was hungry and he wasn't getting anything from me. And I discovered that giving him a bottle of water was a way of calming him down.

But when I mentioned it to a nurse, she said I really shouldn't, because if he was nursing well he didn't need the extra fluid and at the same time it would make it hard to tell from the wetness of his diapers how much he really was nursing.

So I stopped doing that. And the water must have been giving him a false sense of fullness, because as soon as I stopped giving it to him, he started screaming again. It was a nightmare. Within twelve hours, there was nothing I could do to calm him down, not the swing, not holding him. He just screamed and screamed. He cried, and I cried.

Finally I called the doctor, who said, "Sounds like he's hungry. Why don't you give him a bottle for now and bring him in this afternoon so we can see what the problem is."

So I gave him a bottle, and he calmed right down. The difference was incredible. When the doctor checked him, he was under his birth weight, even though by then he was two weeks old, and he seemed dehydrated. So I just put him on the bottle. After a few days, he was an angel.

But it wasn't the end of the feeding problems. I couldn't find a nipple he liked, and for a whole week I was in Toys 'R' Us every single night buying a new kind. I accumulated a huge bag of them, but the only one he really liked was the one that came on the disposable bottles from the hospital. And, of course, you can't buy those anywhere, so I kept reusing the ones I had and going back to Toys 'R' Us. I've never had a harder time solving a stupider problem.

Then I had a problem with the formula. He did fine with the regular, low-iron stuff at first, but after a couple of weeks, he started to have terrible gas pains, and he was crying a lot. My sister-in-law, who's a pediatric nurse, told me about these drops you could buy, but they were very expensive, and I'm not sure whether they worked or not. But I was giving him so much, I decided that it couldn't be that good for him. So she suggested switching to a soy-based formula, and that seemed to do the trick.

■ *Practical Considerations.* Women who simply assume in advance that they will nurse the baby don't realize that breastfeeding is a tremendous commitment. The more traditional your view of motherhood, the easier the commitment is to make. But if you plan to return to work, or if you cherish the idea of splitting child care equally or "fairly" with your husband, nursing may not be the most practical choice.

When you nurse, you become physically attuned to the baby in ways that are beyond your conscious control. The baby's appetite determines how much milk you produce. The baby's sucking or crying, or even your thoughts of the baby when you're separated, determine when the milk starts to flow. The baby, still too young to love you for your own charming personality, comes to appreciate your unique responsiveness to his appetites, and the traces of his appreciation are one of the great rewards in caring for a being who is otherwise undemonstrative.

But your husband may also come to appreciate your unique capacity to respond to the baby's appetite. This means *you* will be up in the middle of the night for most, if not all, feedings. It means that when your husband takes her off your hands for a few moments of respite in the evening, at the first peep she'll be handed back to you with the explanation, "She must be hungry."

It means, in short, that no matter how strong your abstract convictions about sharing responsibility, there is one aspect of the baby's care which you cannot physically share. You can get occasional relief either by pumping relief bottles or supplementing with formula. But the overall responsibility for the baby's care will rest on your shoulders.

If you decide to go back to work full- or part-time, continuing to nurse will be another ball in your juggling act. In addition to worrying about your child care, the general hygienic status of your home, what's getting defrosted for dinner, and whether you're getting enough sleep to perform your job properly, you will also have to worry about whether your milk will let down in the middle of an important meeting and how you're going to squeeze out a serene time for pumping in the office. And you may find that all this worrying decreases your milk supply.

This is a real dilemma for many working mothers. As inconvenient as nursing is, it serves as a physical and psychological way of keeping in touch with the baby when you can't be with him.

Only you can decide how much nursing means to you. But don't keep it up out of guilt. If you love the baby, you'll love her whether you're breast- or bottle-feeding her, and you'll have many more years of opportunities for showing it.

I took a six-week maternity leave from my job, and by the time it was over I found I really looked forward to getting out of the house and seeing other grown-ups and doing some traveling again. I've always made an out-of-town buying trip once a month, and my next one was scheduled for two weeks after I went back.

That's when I discovered I would have to give up nursing, and it broke my heart. It was really important to me to nurse for at least six months, and there was no physical reason why I couldn't.

I tried to keep it up. I left a whole lot of frozen breast milk behind, and when I first got there, I kept pumping and throwing the milk away. But, you know, when you're constantly making sales calls, you can't just excuse yourself in the middle of the call and go pump. So I just stopped, and in a week, my milk was completely gone, with no pain or discomfort.

But it really bothered me. I felt I had blown it as a mother. I thought, "This is the one thing in the world only you can do for him, and you had to go out of town on business." He couldn't have cared less, and I had felt at points that it was pretty cumbersome. But it was also a sign of his dependency on me, and I liked the fact that it was a relationship we had that excluded other people. And I know that, to a certain extent, if I had stayed home with him full-time, it would have been just another process.

My husband stays home and takes care of him while I'm at work. And I don't want to feel that I'm competing with my husband for his affection, but sometimes I do. He gets him all day, but I get him at the end of the day when he's not such fun and he's not so happy, and I'm not such fun and I'm not that happy. And at least when I was nursing, when I came home at night from work, I felt a little more necessary.

When I went back to work part-time at about three months, I thought the hardest problem was going to be dealing with day-care. But it turned out to be dealing with the whole feeding issue.

I tried being a purist. My first few days back at work, I pumped. But I'd spend half an hour and get, like, two ounces, and I just concluded that it was going to take too much time out of my workday and be too confining.

So now I just nurse in the morning and at night, and he gets two bottles during the day. It's working out well now, but for a while, he was screaming at the breast. I guess it was because it's so much easier for him to suck from the bottle. And I think it was confusing for him to have a different schedule every day—to be on bottles certain days, and then nurse when I was at home. So now he gets the same combination of feedings every day, whether I'm giving him the bottles or the sitter is.

But it was hard. I didn't like the idea of the formula at first. When I left him with my husband, I'd call and ask, "So, did he eat it?" And he'd say, "Oh, he loved it; he just slurped it up." And it's awful, because of course you want your kid to eat, but somehow I hoped he'd hate it.

At about five months, I went back to work part-time, about twenty hours a week. At that point, I weaned him, because it was difficult for me to pump the milk. And I wanted to try to lose weight. And I never got comfortable with nursing him in public. He's real distractible, so he'd look around a lot and leave me exposed, and I didn't seem to be able to cover myself up very well.

By that point, I was only nursing twice a day, and giving him two bottles. First, I discontinued the evening feeding, because that's when I was usually at work. And I thought I'd just go on with the one feeding, but there always seemed to be morning meetings and events I had to attend, and he didn't seem to be nursing very well anyway, so I just gave it up.

But it was a hard decision to make, and once I started doing it, I immediately felt, "No, I don't want to do this, I don't want to lose this closeness."

For a couple of weeks, I was quite depressed. But I had read that there were hormonal reasons I might be feeling that way, so I chalked it up to that. And I kept telling myself, "You're just substituting one way of feeding for another, and you have other ways of feeling close to him."

I'm glad now that I did it. It's really much easier for me, and he's getting to the point where he can hold the bottle himself. He never showed any sign of missing the nursing, which surprised me. My husband and I had thought that evening feeding was such an important part of relaxing him to go to sleep. But the bottle did exactly the same thing.

He's four-and-a-half months old, and I've just gone back to work part-time. The days when I'm working are incredibly more stressful than the days when I'm not. I can tell because at work, though I can pump about four or five ounces in the morning, in the afternoons I'm lucky to get two. I'm also a little worried that on those evenings he doesn't really get enough at the ten o'clock feeding to hold him through the night. Until I went back, he seemed to be able to sleep till at least 5:00 in the morning, but now he's getting up at 2:00 or 3:00.

In my building, very few of the offices have doors on them, so I had to make special arrangements with the nurse's office to use one of their rooms. Normally, I take about thirty minutes each morning and afternoon. I just go in, kick off my shoes, get out my picture of the baby, and pump away. Then, because

I'm spending an hour pumping, I always eat lunch at my desk, which I'm sure also isn't great for the milk supply.

The women in the office all know I'm doing it, and they're great. All I have to say to my secretary is, "Back in half an hour." But I think the men had enough trouble with my pregnancy; the last thing I need is to run into them in the halls holding a bottle of breast milk. Through a catalog, I found a very discreet pumping kit that looks like it might be just a purse. Inside, it has a pump and an ice pack that will keep the milk cold for up to a day outside the fridge.

The pump is battery-operated, which I find very efficient. But it's also led to some rather comic scenes on days when I'm too busy to make it all the way down to the nurse's office. If I'm between meetings, I may just have to run into the public restroom. And every time someone comes in, I know they're trying to figure out what this noise is coming from my stall; because I'm getting all tense about the situation, I'm not generally managing to get much milk.

I have to be careful about how I dress. You can't, for example, wear a dress that zips up the back. Now I only wear two-piece things, steer clear of delicate silk blouses, and try to layer things. I've only leaked once in a meeting I couldn't possibly get out of, but luckily I was wearing a turtleneck with a sweater over it. It didn't come through on the sweater, but the shirt was soaked and I spent half an hour afterwards in the ladies' room with a hair dryer trying to dry it off.

▪ *Emotional Concerns.*   The way to a baby's heart is through his stomach. Your mother and mother-in-law know this, even though in their day it wasn't trendy to talk about "profoundly fulfilling feeding experiences"—that's why they keep asking if they can give the baby a bottle or a little solid food. It's why husbands who consciously support the idea of breast-feeding often make off-handed remarks that seem to undermine it. Sensing their jealousy, mothers often describe nursing as satisfying because it's something "only I can do for the baby."

The tide of public opinion has turned very much against those women who are neutral on the subject, or who feel uncomfortable with or burdened by breast-feeding. If you weren't wild about sharing your body throughout pregnancy, it may come as a shock that nursing means surrendering it for another year or more. In the meantime, you will be warned not to diet, not to drink or smoke much if at all, and not to take drugs of any kind. You may find that you are disturbed by the erotic feelings nursing can arouse. Or you may be unhappy about the size or behavior of your previously ornamental assets.

Any of these reasons may sound trivial to someone else. But if your feelings about nursing aren't largely positive, there's no point in continuing simply because it's the thing to do. If being a loving mother is the issue, it may be more important for you to feel good about your life and your body, and to show your love for the baby in other ways.

I wasn't really into the idea of nursing to start with. I figured I'd try it, but I didn't think I could handle the physical sensation of someone sucking at my breast. It seemed very sexual. But it turned out that I didn't feel a thing. There was no physical feeling at all, nor did it make me feel any closer to her.

But I gave up after three weeks. I had inverted nipples, and she couldn't grab on right. She'd keep looking for it, and it would be in her mouth. And she seemed to have jaws of steel. So I started dreading feedings, counting how many more I'd have to get through in the day. Finally, I just called the pediatrician and said, "I'm switching to bottles." And he said, "Fine." And she's been content ever since.

I just stopped cold, and it hurt a lot. I thought, "If you've only been nursing for three weeks, how much milk could you have?" I stopped on a Friday, and Saturday I was in incredible pain. I tried ice packs and aspirin, and nothing helped. I tried to release a little by pumping, but I couldn't get anything. I was sure I'd get a breast infection. But by Sunday I was getting more comfortable, and by Monday I fit into my old bra and felt fine.

Recommended Reading

Bottlefeeding Without Guilt: A Reassuring Guide for Loving Parents by Peggy Robin. Prima Publishing, Calif., 1996.

The Complete Book of Breastfeeding by Marvin S. Eiger, M.D., and Sally Wendkos Olds. Workman, New York, 1987.

The Nursing Mother's Companion by Kathleen Huggins. Harvard Common Press, Boston, 1995.

The Nursing Mother's Guide to Weaning by Kathleen Huggins and Linda Ziedrich. Harvard Common Press, Boston, 1994.

The Womanly Art of Breastfeeding by La Leche League International. Plume, New York, 1991.

seven

Ideal *The baby will sleep peacefully in a basket for the first few months, while you get your body back in shape, cook gourmet meals, and learn to play the violin.*
Fact *Just feeding and diapering a newborn takes all day. If the baby is colicky, you'll be overachieving if you get your thank-you notes written before he's sitting up.*

When you were pregnant, you heard the dire warning over and over: "You won't believe how much your life changes after you have a baby." And now you know. For years, you realize, you just took it for granted that adults slept eight hours a night, that every evening they sat down to decently prepared food and made interesting conversation, that a "good" day was one on which you could tell somebody proudly, "Today I accomplished x, y, and z."

One of the really depressing aspects of the first weeks with a new infant is that it's hard to sort out which of the changes that have swept over your life like a tidal wave are permanent, and which will recede. Actually, while you'll never again be exactly the person you were before, your life isn't going to stay focused forever on eating, sleeping, and eliminating—any more than your baby's will.

The route your baby can be expected to take out into the world is well documented; a book such as T. Berry Brazelton's *Infants and*

Mothers is good to have around if you're interested in knowing how infants normally develop month-by-month through the first year (with gentle suggestions on some aspects of child care). *The First Twelve Months of Life,* by Frank Caplan, contains similar information.

But what about *your* life? What, for a new mother, makes a "good" day? When will you be able to count on sleeping through the night again, or taking the baby to a restaurant without fearing she'll scream through the meal, or simply grabbing an hour and a half to yourself during the day to relax with a book (or clean the toilet, if you will)?

Unfortunately, no one can tell you *exactly* when. Some babies sleep through the night regularly at six weeks, and some hardly do at all for the first year or more. Some take long, reliable naps, allowing you, for instance, to run a business from home with little or no baby-sitting, while some absolutely refuse to nap at all, making even a sociable phone call difficult.

What makes the first weeks especially hard for many women is the sense that, in struggling to regain control over their lives, they are fighting almost impossible odds. For this reason, I asked women at various stages of the first year to describe a "typical" day with their babies. The resulting stories may offer you two forms of reassurance.

The first is that, as Marie discovered on her second night home from the hospital, when the odds *are* all stacked against you, surrendering control may be the surest route to sanity. The second, as the other stories prove, is that the total dependence of infancy doesn't last forever.

Old Wives' Tales

At Three Weeks

"I Can't See How Anyone Could Do This Alone."

The very first weeks are overwhelming for almost everyone. The baby is on no particular schedule, waking up when you'd rather be sleeping, overflowing diapers as fast as you can change them, eating and eating and eating. Your main challenge is just to keep up with it all, and you'll need the help of a husband and/or mother and/or friend to do it.

Marie, twenty-nine, is on a two-month maternity leave from her job as an attorney. Her husband, Danny, is working on his Ph.D. and is home during the day. He had planned to take care of the baby full-time after Marie returned to work, while continuing to write his dissertation, but they are having second thoughts about this arrangement now that they realize how demanding a baby is.

Like most mothers at the three-week point. Marie is still very occupied with her own and her baby's physical needs. Down from the initial euphoria of the birth, she has definitely felt the impact of new strains on her life, and is just beginning to think about how she may cope.

Last night the seven o'clock feeding was on the left breast. We're keeping a record of which breast does what feeding, because in the later part of the day when both breasts feel empty, I can never figure out which breast is less empty. He finished about 7:15, and then I think he lay in bed and looked at his mobile while I put pictures of him into a photo album.

There was another feeding from 9:00 till 9:05, but I think he might have spit up most of that. We watched a PBS special on Simon and Garfunkel—even though we've noticed that he won't really go to sleep while the TV's on—because we were bored. There was another feeding from 10:45 to 10:52, which wasn't very long by his standards. Feedings are usually about fifteen minutes.

Around eleven o'clock, I turned the baby over to Danny and I conked out. I think they were up for another hour. The baby really does seem to have settled down at night during the past week. He doesn't require much jiggling and entertaining between feedings, whereas during the day he'll stay up an hour, if not three or four.

There was another feeding around 3:00 A.M., and I know I got some pretty good sleep because I was dreaming long dreams with plots, which I've just started doing again the last few nights. So, between that and the nap I'd taken the afternoon before, I felt pretty good for that feeding, whereas usually I feel so ornery in the middle of the night that Danny has to hold the baby while I prepare mentally and go to the bathroom and wriggle around on the bed to find a good position and swear a little.

I feed him, and then I kick Danny and tell him the baby needs changing, and then I have to see whether he wants to eat more to calm down, because he usually gets so riled up being changed. But after a couple of sips, he usually falls back asleep. So then I put him back in his basket.

He was up again about quarter to seven, tossing and turning and grunting like a piglet, making all these noises which we've now come to understand don't necessarily mean he's hungry. So we don't pick him up right away, because sometimes you do that, and he takes a few sips, and there you are, upright and awake, while meanwhile the baby's gone back to sleep for another half hour.

So I let him fuss a little, but then gave him another feeding around 7:00 A.M. He was a little more fussy this time, and I was afraid he was going to decide it was daytime now and not go back to sleep. He did go back to sleep, but he wouldn't go into his basket, so Danny had to take him into bed with us. This has happened a couple of times in the morning, and sometimes it's the only way he'll sleep at night. I'm grateful when Danny just takes over like that, because it means I can just turn my brain off for a while and go back to sleep for another three hours.

So then he slept till about 9:50, and then there was another longish feeding. This is Sunday morning now. And after this feeding, I know he's going to wake up and be really alert and we all really have to get going. Now, at every feeding, with the possible exception of the 7:00 A.M. one, I ask Danny to get me something to drink. It's been very hot and humid here, and we're not eating at regular times, so I have to make sure to keep my fluid intake up. Also with each feeding, there's at least one change. We try to change him before the feeding, but then afterwards he's so relaxed that he'll poop.

So after the feeding, I took a shower and Danny changed him and walked him around the house, showing him pictures. He's very interested in paintings and in his mobile. He especially likes Picasso, I think because the colors are very bright and everything's outlined in black.

He stayed up most of the morning. Occasionally he'd sort of drift off but then wake again, but he didn't really take a nap till after the 12:30 feeding. We keep this record of all the feedings, and we've notice over the course of today that the feedings yesterday and today are almost exactly the same. He's doing about eight altogether.

But we're not eating terribly well. I mean, we're tying to eat vegetables and everything, but it's just not happening on a regular basis. Last night for dinner we had stewed tomatoes and cranberry juice and cheese sandwiches. This morning we ate the remains of a blueberry pie, two pieces each, and we just had cheese sandwiches again for lunch.

But I did make the bed after breakfast. And we had the Sunday newspaper, but you can't really read it while you're trying to hold the baby.

I feel a little nuts when I think about all the things I have to do and the tiny bit of time I have to do anything. I've been trying to put this photograph album together and send copies of this one picture to some of our friends and write some letters, and the hospital bill came yesterday, so I had to ask Danny to go to the bank to switch some money around in the accounts. And I hate the fact that I have to ask him to do all these things for me.

It can be very hard to have guests around, but it depends on the guests. Tonight two friends of mine from work are stopping by, and we don't really know if they're expecting food—or if they'll bring some. It's a little scary to have people around that time of day because that's when the baby's usually noisy, and you don't want to have to spend all your time just trying to keep him quiet. But we know they even hired a sitter for their own two kids so they could come, so we don't want it to be too awful.

If the guest is someone very close, and we can all just kind of lie around, it's fine. But even that was really hard at the very beginning. My family was here, and I wanted to have them, but I didn't want to get out of bed or talk or anything. I was just so exhausted, and there were so many of them.

The first day after I got back from the hospital, this friend from work I really like came over, and I had this incredible—I think hormonal—reaction. She and Danny were trying to put together the swing, and I heard them out in the living room laughing. I got so upset because I couldn't go out there with them, but I was exhausted. But that was only the first few days. After that, the people I like, I wanted to have over. The people I didn't like, I figured I just had to put up with.

It's been kind of frustrating not really being able to get out. The first week, I might have pushed the stroller around in the little park next to our building, but that was all I could physically do. The second week, I overdid it. I went to a mall and did all these errands, and then I felt like my insides were falling out. So I lay low for a few days after that.

The nursing can be frustrating, too. The first few days I felt this awful despair about having to feed all hours of the day and night. I was exhausted and run-down. The first day I came home from the hospital, my breasts got engorged and we bought a little pump to try to release some pressure. That whole first week, my nipples were very, very sore. So I got some nipple shields, but I couldn't stand the way they felt, and I didn't think the baby liked the rubber, and I don't think they took the pressure off that much, so I never really used them. But at times it's hurt so much, I found myself using the Lamaze techniques to stand the pain. Sometimes the baby is in a really antsy mood, and he'll start pulling and thrashing at the nipple.

I think what really upset me at the beginning was the unpredictability. I remember very clearly a feeding in the middle of the night the second night back from the hospital, when maybe the hormones were already going back to normal or something, and it suddenly hit me, "You just have to put up with it, and if you put up with it, everything will be all right." It was terrible to have to do, but it was much better once I did it.

I feel okay about the amount of sleep I'm getting, especially if I can get a nap in the afternoon. I feel like I can count on enough two- or three-hour blocks of sleep at night, as long as Danny takes him at the end of that fussy period. But I can't see how anyone could do this alone.

He's a really good baby, though. I like him a lot. I like it when he looks like he's sated with milk; that makes me feel really good. And I like looking down at his face while he's sucking and his eyes are wide open and he's looking around the room. I feel like we communicate with sounds. Sometimes he makes this little humming noise, and we hum together.

I'm very preoccupied about how I'm going to be able to go back to work. I hate the fact that someone else is going to have to take care of the baby. I know Danny can do it part of the time, but now that I know how much time it really takes, I see that it was unreasonable to think he could do it and get anything else done at the same time.

I'm just amazed how nobody can really tell you how consuming this is. People can tell you till they're blue in the face how it takes all your energy, but you still don't understand what they mean until you feel all your energy gone.

At Eight Weeks

"Is It Possible to Exercise and Get Dressed, All in the Same Morning?"

Somewhere around the six-week point, many women find that coping with the baby—and life in general—becomes noticeably easier. For one thing, although you won't be back to your pre-pregnancy energy level, your body has had a chance to recover. For another, the baby is by now somewhat better organized and capable of doing longer stretches between feedings and at night—possibly even sleeping through. He's smiling sociably and making eye contact, two accomplishments which sound minor but which may dramatically increase your joy and confidence in mothering.

Frances, thirty-seven, is under a great deal of pressure. A college professor, she is teaching one night a week, tending to her own consulting company, and moving into a new house— all without any dependable form of baby-sitting. Fortunately, her son Toby is usually calm and relatively independent.

At eight weeks, Frances is beginning to see that life will fall back into place. She can get out with the baby to do errands, has found a part-time day-care arrangement, which will begin in another month, and gets through the long, crowded days at home without feeling that she wants to hurl Toby into her husband's arms the instant he walks in the door. She thinks wistfully of her old efficiency, but she has also developed a smaller and more reasonable set of expectations for things she can accomplish while being a mother.

He's not on any kind of schedule, so there's really no such thing as a "typical" day. On my typical day, all I'm trying to do is enjoy the baby, meet his needs, and get one thing accomplished, whether that's work I do in the house or I make it out to a meeting.

Usually, he'll wake up between 5:00 and 6:00 A.M. People say that means he's slept through the night, but it's not enough to keep me from feeling sleep deprived the next day.

Anyway, usually I get up with him at that point, and my rule is that if I can deal with what he needs then within an hour, I won't wake Jim. But if it takes more than an hour, we play baby-hand-off and I go wake him up and say, "He's yours, I need another hour of sleep."

I also deal with him if he's up in the middle of the night, which he still sometimes is, just because it's easier for me to nurse at that point than to wander downstairs for a bottle. Once he gets fed, he'll pretty much go right back to sleep; for a while he wouldn't, but I think he just wasn't getting enough to eat. Last night, he was still awake when I put him back in his crib, and I just gave him his pacifier, turned on the music box, patted him on the back, and went back to bed. And he went back to sleep on his own.

Anyway, he rarely wakes up in the middle of the night unless he's fallen asleep too early in the day. I've often thought it would be smart to wake him up at 10:00 or 11:00 P.M. and give him an extra feeding, but if I've been up since 5:00 myself, I'm way too tired to take the risk that he might not want to go back to sleep again. He's also really hard to feed while he's sleepy.

So then he gets up between 5:00 and 6:00 A.M., and I usually start out breast-feeding him, but then I might give him a bottle, too. We never gave him the luxury of a warm bottle, so he's used to drinking it straight from the refrigerator.

At the beginning, it really worried me that I had no idea how much formula he was supposed to be drinking. But then I learned to just trust that he was taking as much as he needed. Also I learned to tell which cry means he's hungry. The cry when he wants to eat starts out sounding just like a normal baby cry, and then turns into a full-blown wail and he might turn kind of purple if he's not satisfied. I think he's eating five or six times a day, maybe about thirty-two ounces of formula, plus breast-feedings.

Anyway, after that first feeding, he might go right back to sleep, or stay up for an hour, but very happily. When he's awake, he just kind of hangs out. He looks around and looks at lights, and gurgles and plays with his hands. He actually has the capacity to entertain himself for forty-five minutes to an hour—not that he always does, but he can. And after the first hour in the morning, he usually goes back to sleep.

So the challenge for the morning is: Is it possible to exercise and get dressed, all in the same morning? In the last few weeks, I've been trying to get back to my old exercise routine, which takes between an hour and an hour and a half. Before the baby, I'd get up at 6:00 A.M. and do it till 7:30, and then it would take another forty-five minutes to shower and do my hair and get dressed. But now the exercising is usually interrupted by some phone calls related to work, and I end up doing other little things that need doing, and usually my "hour and a half" may end up stretching out till 10:00 A.M.

So if I know I'll have to be somewhere at 10:00, for instance, I'll sacrifice the exercise, because I know I have to use the opportunity to get dressed. But if we're staying home, and he wants to eat again after I'm through exercising, I might never get dressed.

I also try to straighten up the house in the morning, and if I need to go grocery shopping, the supermarket is only a block or so away. So usually I'll wait till after he's eaten and he's happy, and then I'll put him in the Snugli and he'll sleep through it.

My own meals seem to get sacrificed or squished into other things. I find myself making irrational decisions to eat lunch really early because suddenly I have the time, or realizing at three o'clock that I haven't gotten to it yet. The books say that when you bottle-feed, you're supposed to hold the baby to give him the same sense of closeness he'd get from nursing. But sometimes the only time I have to eat is when he's eating, so I'll just put him in his chair and give him his bottle with one hand and use the other hand to eat my own lunch.

My challenge for the afternoons is to try to figure out how to get him outside for a little while, and accomplish something else, like unpacking some boxes or doing some work. Right now, I don't have consistent baby-sitting, although I will in another month, so sometimes just arranging for sitting so I can work later is a job in itself.

I didn't take him out much for the first month or so, because life just seemed too complicated and I was in a sort of daze. Now

I take him, but I worry a lot about how to time it right. The only time I actually wake him up to feed him is when I know we're going somewhere where it's going to be inconvenient for him to eat.

The thing is, errands that would have seemed easy before the baby have become ridiculously complicated. For instance, last week, I had to get my oil changed. So, to be smart and save time, instead of going to my regular mechanic halfway across town, I decided to go to this place right around the corner. It takes them about an hour to do it, so before the baby, I would have dropped the car off around 1:00, been back home in fifteen minutes or so, worked all afternoon, and picked the car up around 5:00.

This is what happened. First, you don't want him to go hysterical on you. You don't want to have to nurse at the service station. So I got him up and fed him, and after that, it was about 1:45. Then I put the car seat in the car, so I could drive him, and the Snugli, so I could walk him home. So we drove there, and I took him with me in the seat to make the arrangements, which took about ten minutes, and then had to take him back to the car, put the seat back, put the Snugli on, and get him into it. Then I thought I'd take him for a walk while they did it. But then after the walk he needed a diaper change, so I ended up taking him home and changing him, and then he needed to eat again. Then, when we got back to the station, they had trouble finding the car, so we hung around for fifteen minutes or so, and then just paying is a huge logistical hassle when you have this bundle strapped across the whole front of your body. Then I had to take him back to the car, get him out of the Snugli, get him into the car seat, get the Snugli off me, and drive home again. So we still ended up home around 5:00, but all I had managed to accomplish was changing the oil.

These days I find myself making lots of lists, which I've never done before. And they have to be very specific lists. I can't just say "Clean the kitchen," I have to say, "Wash kitchen floor," so I'll be able to cross it off. Or I can't say, "Write thank-you notes," I have to say, "Write five thank-you notes." That's the only way I find I can have a sense of accomplishment.

We're fairly casual about dinner. Jim isn't the kind of husband who expects to find it on the table when he comes home. I might decide I *want* to make something, although since the baby I haven't made anything that takes more than about twenty minutes to prepare. Or else he'll call and ask if he should pick something up on the way home.

Jim usually gets home around 7:00 or 7:30 P.M. In the beginning, I was hysterically desperate for him to get home, but over the past few weeks that's changed. I was feeling very resentful that he wasn't coming home earlier, but, as he pointed out to me, if he came home an hour earlier, it really wouldn't help me significantly. When he does get home, he really takes over, and sometimes I worry that's not really fair, because he works all day, too. But he seems to be able to stay up later than I can.

I'm not sure why we turned a corner. I think part of what made me so hysterical at the end of the day was that the whole day was so frustrating. And now that I'm starting to organize my life, I don't have quite as much anxiety.

Around 4:00 or 5:00 P.M., Toby will eat, and then sleep another few hours. But I'm always wondering what the pattern is going to be. Is he going to eat early enough, like around three, so that by the time he wakes up, he can stay up for a while and then go to sleep sometime reasonable, like around 10:00? The ideal thing is when he's up from around 6:00 till 9:00 or 10:00. But there's only about a 40 percent chance of that.

There are bad evenings. Last night, Jim had to work till about 9:00, and I'd figured I could get a little bit of work done in the evening. But the baby woke up at 5:30 and screamed and screamed. He ate for a long time, till about 6:30, and then he was perfectly happy till about 8:00 when he started screaming again. I figured he wanted to eat again, so I nursed him, and he kept screaming, so I figured I didn't have enough milk. So I tried the bottle, and he started eating as though he really wanted to be eating, but then he started screaming again. So I thought, "Maybe it's the nipple." So I got a new nipple and tried again, and that didn't work. So I thought, "Maybe it's the formula." So I got a new bottle with new formula. And that did it.

I have no idea what was really bothering him. I don't know if these were growing pains or his stomach hurt or he was un-happy with something I gave him. But it just stopped, and then he was perfectly pleasant. But by then it was about 9:30, and between 5:30 and 9:30 I was doing nothing but attending to his needs.

I don't worry about getting him to sleep at a particular time. I wait till I hear his sleepy cry, which isn't really a real cry, but it's a sort of fussy-whiny cry. Sometimes it's a false alarm, and I'll put him in the crib and he'll start screaming, and then I might feed him or sing a song. But usually when he does that kind of fussing, I'll just lay him down on his stomach. He really seems to need some quiet time to himself. He can handle that. Sometimes he'll kick and flail a little, but as long as he doesn't cry, I figure he's just working off his excess energy, and I let him handle it. If he actually cries, I pick him up.

I find it extremely comforting that I can read his signals pretty well. The first few weeks, I really couldn't, but now I really feel that he communicates what he wants to me.

But I wish I weren't under so much pressure. I always feel I have to be getting something done. And I do. If you have your own consulting business, you can't just put it on hold, because you may not have a business to go back to. If I want to have work four months from now, I've got to talk to potential clients and write proposals now.

I know a lot of women who've said when they've had a child that for this period of this baby's life, just caring for the baby and maybe the house was going to be their full-time occupation, and they weren't going to feel guilty about not doing anything else. And before I had a baby, I couldn't imagine wanting that. But now I think it would be very nice to have four or five months of just doing that.

The only time I just feel like a blissful mom is on weekends. I had thought that with my husband home then I'd do my work on weekends and he'd have some time alone with the baby. But I've found that I really like being with both Jim and the baby. Otherwise, if all we were doing was trading off child care, we'd never just be a family.

At Six Months

"A Much Mommier Day than Usual . . ."

Trish, twenty-eight, has been running a free-lance business out of her home since the baby, Nicole, was only a few weeks old. So far, she's managed it with no baby-sitting, working through Nicole's long naps and, as she admits, sometimes ignoring her for long stretches of the morning while she makes phone calls. A baby who doesn't nap, cries constantly when not being held or amused, or still wakes up for lots of night feedings would probably make this arrangement impossible, but Nicole sleeps well and seems very happy to amuse herself for long stretches of time, and Trish hasn't been overloaded with work.

This isn't to say that the early months were a breeze. Trish was surprised by how hard her physical recovery was, and during the weeks she was up regularly in the middle of the night, she found it hard to concentrate on work during the day. And she found it tremendously frustrating that she often couldn't identify any reason for Nicole's crying, and couldn't calm it.

At six months, Trish feels she has regained a great deal of control over her life. She started out breast-feeding on demand but is now beginning to feed Nicole grown-up food on a grown-up schedule. She can take Nicole to restaurants and on errands without worrying much about leaking diapers, screaming fits, or sudden feeding pit-stops.

While her life has certainly stretched to accommodate Nicole's needs, it's also clear that she's relieved because she understands those needs better. She knows what affects Nicole's napping and when Nicole doesn't like a particular food. She also knows that Nicole is becoming in some ways *more* demanding as she become more mobile, and that Trish will soon have to give up working and "Mommying" simultaneously.

Last night she went to bed at 7:30. But I made a mistake. Yesterday, we changed her eating schedule. She used to get a bottle when she woke up; cereal and a bottle four hours later; vegetables and a bottle four hours later; fruit, cereal, and a bottle four hours later. But we decided we wanted to make her eat more like a real person. so yesterday morning, we gave her a real breakfast of cereal and a bottle, in her high chair, right when she woke up, around 7:00. Then, around noon, she got her vegetable and a bottle. Then, between 4:00 and 5:00 P.M. she got cereal again and a bottle. And normally, I'd give her a fourth bottle as a nightcap, just before she went to bed. But I forgot.

So she woke up at 4:30 this morning, which is very rare. She always sleeps from 7:00 P.M. to 7:00 A.M. except when she's had a vaccination. She was up maybe twenty minutes, but I didn't go in. I could hear her, but she wasn't really crying and she didn't sound mad or upset. Normally, she's not a ravenously hungry baby, so I figured she'd probably be okay. But I felt terribly guilty that I'd forgotten that bottle.

And when Mike fed her this morning at 7:15, she had a big breakfast, a lot of cereal and milk. Then we packed her up at quarter to eight and took her out to a coffee shop for breakfast. That's not normal for us; we hardly ever take her out in the morning, although we used to go to breakfast when we were young, working people, especially on Fridays. She sat in the high chair and made lots of friends. She gave big smiles to everyone who came by, charming them. We gave her a spoon we'd soaked in cold water, and she sucked on the edge of it. She threw her toy down on the floor about fifty times.

Then I put her in the car seat and drove to the supermarket and shopped. She slept in the backpack, which I knew meant trouble because I wouldn't be able to get her to take a real morning nap at home. She's not a very good napper.

We got home between 9:30 and 10:00. I put her in the playpen while I unpacked the groceries and talked on the phone. She's very good in the playpen. She plays with toys and she's still fascinated by the mobile that plays Brahms' "Lullaby."

Around 11:00 A.M., a potential baby-sitter came by with her two children for an interview. They stayed maybe an hour, and by the time they left she was kvetching. So I fed her lunch, and that knocked her out. Oh, and we had a little fight over lunch, because even though normally she has no trouble with squash and sweet potatoes, she was so wound up that every time I tried to feed her, she'd tighten up her lips and turn away. So I decided to try small-curd cottage cheese, which the doctor had recommended. And I could tell that, despite her mood, she actually liked it. At least, she wasn't clamping her mouth shut. But she's still not that interested in trying something new and she really wanted her bottle. She finished it, and as soon as I put her into the crib she fell asleep.

By now it was 12:30 or 12:45. Normally, as soon as she's in the crib, I run to the word processor. Actually, normally I ignore her for most of the morning to get my work done. But that's getting to be impossible because she's getting so much more mobile, which is why I'm looking for a sitter a few days a week now.

Today I had a much mommier day than usual. I didn't do any work at all. When she went to asleep, I just put my feet up on the coffee table and read magazines. Then I took a thirty-minute nap, and it was about 1:30, which is when my play group meets. And since it only goes for a few hours, I wanted to get going. So I made some noise, and finally around 2:00 P.M. she woke up, screaming.

She still probably needs three or more hours a day of sleep, and I hadn't given her enough. But I changed her and dressed her and packed her up and went.

It was very pleasant. It was in a big house, and we had cookies and chatted. Some of these women have known each other since Lamaze class, and the play group had been meeting for quite a while before I joined. But they were very welcoming.

Now, during play group, I think it must be noted that she was not a happy camper. She was kvetching and nothing was making her quite happy, even though normally she likes just crawling around and chomping on other babies' toys. Anyway, around 4:00 P.M. I fed her dinner in someone else's car seat—Gerber's peaches, which I brought with me, and Enfamil, which I measure into the bottle ahead of time and just add tap water.

Then we left, and she fell asleep in the car. Then I thought, since she hadn't had a lot of sleep and I didn't want to wake her right up again, that I'd drive around for a while. So I took a real gamble. Now, you might think I'm a bad mother for doing this, but I went to a shopping center, pulled right up to the video store so I'd be able to see her from the window, and went in. I locked the door very carefully, and I made sure it wasn't too cold, and I kept checking on her.

When I came out, she was still sleeping, so I decided to drive past the house of the baby-sitter I'd interviewed, just to check her out. I got home around 5:30. She woke up when the car stopped, so I took her up and put her in the playpen while I looked at the mail and called back some people who'd left messages about the baby-sitter ad.

Meanwhile, Mike came home, and he played with her for an hour and gave her a bottle while I made dinner. We decided to try to keep her up a little later, so we could all three of us have a sit-down dinner, like we haven't done in I-can't-even-tell-you-how-long. So around 7:00 we sat down at the table, with her in her high chair, but she was tired and crabby, and obviously it wasn't going to be a nice quiet dinner. So I picked her up, had her say good night to Daddy, and put her in the crib, and that was the last we heard of her, around 7:15.

At Nine Months

"Guess What! We're Going to Walgreen's!"

Suzy was a colicky baby, and Wendy wasn't sure, in the first three months, that she was going to survive motherhood. Philosophically, she was absolutely committed to being a full-time mother, but the days at home were very long, and she sometimes felt she hated the baby. Some afternoons, she'd call her husband at the office and say, "She's screaming, and I can't stand it anymore. Would you please come and just take her away from me."

At nine months, Suzy shows absolutely no trace of her early agony. She is bright, calm, and sometimes flirtatious. Whereas once Wendy did necessary errands grimly and as fast as possible, praying that Suzy would stay quiet, she now dawdles, delighting in Suzy's curiosity about the world around her. No longer is Suzy someone Wendy simply cares for; she can also be, at times, a companion.

She gets up between 5:45 and 6:15 A.M. and gets a bottle while I hold her. She holds the bottle, so I've tried to read while she drinks, but she always tries to grab the book. So I'll take a newspaper and turn it to what I want to read and put it where she can't see it. That way I can read something, but I can't flip through it.

Then I might let her crawl around, play with toys, stand up at the coffee table. She lives for standing up right now, so I might just clear everything out of the way and let her do that.

Then I'll put her into bed with my husband, and she'll wake him up and play with him, and I'll go swimming from 7:00 to 8:00. Meanwhile, he'll put her in her chair and take her into the bathroom so she can watch him shave and sit there while he showers. And he'll feed her some cereal and fruit.

Around 8:15 A.M., she gets juice mixed with water, and then she goes down for a nap till about 10:00. I'll spend the time straightening up. People have told me I should lighten up about that. And I wouldn't say I'm terribly meticulous. I'm sure I never wash the kitchen floor more often than every two weeks. But there's always Stuff all over the place. I've tried to lighten up and not worry about it for a few days, but then I look around me and the bed's not made and there's junk all over the floor, and that really depresses me to have to live with.

During her morning nap, I never do anything nice for myself, like read. If I'm not straightening up, I'll make her formula, or make her baby food and freeze it. Sometimes I'm not sure what I do with that time. Isn't that horrible? On my good days, that strikes me as funny, but on my bad days, it makes me want to cry.

Around 10:00 A.M. she gets up, and I give her a bath. Then I do errands or go out to visit someone. She's very good about being out. She looks around at everything, and I think she thinks I'm doing it all just to entertain her. The nice thing about being a stay-at-home mom is that I have the time to dawdle and make it fun for her. And that's also why on the bad days I cry. You know you're in trouble when you tell the baby, "Guess what! Today we're going to Walgreen's!" and that's going to be the highlight of your day.

Since she holds her own bottle, I just let her eat in the car. But whatever I do, I always stop at 12:00 to give her a vegetable and a fruit. And I get her home by 1:30, because then she needs to take another nap, and if I let her fall asleep even for ten minutes in the car, that's all the nap she'll take.

At this nap, she'll sleep an hour or an hour and a half, and I will try to read something, or maybe I'll just sack out. Or someone will call. I've noticed that people have assumed that because I'm home I just want to talk forever on the phone, but that nap is the only time I ever get to myself, and I don't want to talk. I've started unplugging the phones.

She wakes up between 3:30 and 4:00 and gets another bottle. And by that point, you can think, "All right, Jake is going to be home pretty soon." If she gets up on the early side, I might take her to the park, or walk to a food store that's about four blocks from the house. Or if I don't go to the park and I'm not cooking, I might just hang out on the floor with her and watch her crawl. Yesterday, we had to be somewhere in the morning, so it was in the afternoon that I straightened up.

I might also sew in the late afternoon. I can put her in the playpen for maybe twenty minutes at a time, and she'll just practice standing up. I sew one seam at a time, and leave the stuff out for a week and get to it whenever I can. It might take me a whole week to sew six seams. But at least it's something I can do when she's awake. You can't read when a baby's awake.

But mostly, by that point, I'm just waiting for Jake to come home. I always have this feeling that he's going to come in and change my life. Which is a big burden to put on someone else, I guess. You know how tomato plants look after the rain, when they're not up on sticks? That's how I am when Jake comes home.

I only manage to make dinner twice a week or so. To cook, I have to put her in the playpen, but she's usually ornery by then because it's getting close to her bedtime. Or I might just let her crawl around on the kitchen floor, but she'll climb up the backs of my legs. Sometimes I make dinner holding her.

The other nights, Jake brings something home or we go out for those quickie, forty-minute, $3.95 cheapie dinners. It's become a joke with us: He calls and says, "Hi, I'll be home by six-thirty." And I say, "Okay, and I won't have dinner for you."

So between 6:00 and 6:30 P.M. he comes home, and we'll all play together for a while. We'll start to wind her down for bed, change her, do the foot exercises we're supposed to do because her feet are crooked. Then I feed her around 7:00, and she's out by 7:30. Four nights a week, I'll put her to bed, and three nights, he will.

Then I usually don't feel like doing anything. I might straighten out the mess she's made, or we might wolf down something Jake has brought home if we haven't gotten to it yet. Five nights a week, we end up eating off the coffee table, sitting on the floor. Then there's bill paying, or someone calls, and before you know it, it's 10:00. On weekends, we might rent a video—but we might not be able to stay up late enough to finish watching it.

P.S.: Life with a Colicky Baby Is Different

If the preceding stories depressed you—especially the first two; if they struck you as ridiculously easy; if your own life is simply a struggle to carve out a few moments of calm and quiet from otherwise mercilessly frenetic days and nights; if, in short, your baby is colicky, you deserve a great deal more sympathy and comfort than anyone is likely to give you.

A colicky baby cries a lot. Most of the time, you think. It usually starts out late in the afternoon and may go on far into the night. At first it sounds like normal, fretful crying. Then it escalates to a forlorn wail, and then to a piercing shriek. The small body stiffens, the tiny fists clench, the face goes first red, then purple. You have changed, fed, burped, and bounced this infant, and can think of nothing else to do. So you hold the little body close to your own, walking for as long as your arms and legs hold out. You know that, after a few hours, this is going to suddenly and mercifully stop. You also know that not too long after that, it will start all over again.

The good news is: Colicky babies aren't "sick." Whatever it is that makes them cry like that won't keep them from gaining weight magnificently and hitting all the proper developmental milestones on schedule. And they're not crying because of anything you're doing wrong. Colicky infants the world over cry like this for about three (occasionally four or five) months and then stop.

Here's the bad news: Three months is a *very* long time when you're living with a infant who cries as though being starved and tortured when in fact he is bountifully fed and constantly caressed. Colic is a terrifying introduction to parenthood, guaranteed to make you and your husband feel helpless, incompetent, and exhausted. And the unfortunate fact is that there's no safe, reliable "cure" other than waiting it out until that magical point when the baby simply outgrows it.

▪ *What Is Colic?* The main symptoms of colic are the particular kind of inconsolable, piercing crying described above and the fact that it occurs frequently, not occasionally. Dr. Marc Weissbluth, pediatrician, father, and author of *Crybabies—Coping with Colic: What to Do When Baby Won't Stop Crying*, defines it as "inconsolable crying for which no physical cause can be found, which lasts more than three hours a day, occurs at least three days a week and continues for at least three weeks."

▪ *What Causes Colic?* Amazingly, even in late-twentieth-century America, researchers can't figure it out. Among the factors they have examined and dismissed are: birth order, sex, fetal hiccuping, length of pregnancy, style of childbirth ("natural" or medically assisted), style of feeding (breast or bottle), tendency toward diarrhea or constipation, and willingness of parents to comfort or let the baby cry it out. Factors the researchers still take seriously include: allergies (to formula or something in the breast milk), immaturity of the nervous system, sleep disorders, inability of the digestive tract to properly process food and gas, and insufficient ability to produce hormones or enzymes that aid digestion.

One long-discredited notion that refuses to die is that colic is a manifestation of the anxiety sensitive babies pick up from nervous, first-time parents. This accusation is usually devastating to shell-shocked mommies and daddies who, if they weren't overanxious to start with, certainly haven't gained self-confidence from their exposure to unsoothable infants.

Researchers have found, however, that colic is just as likely to strike second, third, or fourth babies—whose parents presumably already know what they're doing. And studies designed to measure the emotional stability of mothers of colicky babies have shown them to be no more neurotic or tense than the mothers of non-colicky babies.

One thing is clear: Nothing under your control could have kept your baby from developing colic.

■ *What Can You Do About It?* The first thing you want to do is have your doctor diagnose it, just so you're *sure* there's no other medical condition involved. Since allergies and lactose intolerance may produce symptoms similar to those of colic, don't be surprised if he or she suggests changing formulas or if you're nursing, eliminating certain foods from your diet. On the other hand, don't be surprised if none of this works. Statistically, the chances are slight that the baby's problems are feeding related. But anything that *might* work is always worth trying.

One note on dealing with doctors: For a variety of reasons, doctors don't always deal supportively with colic. It's not life threatening and as yet has no cure, so there's not much, medically speaking, they can do about it. If they belong to a crowded practice, they may not feel they have much time for sympathetic listening, and if they've never lived with colic themselves, they may not understand the enormous strain it puts on the parents.

If you're lucky, you'll be getting enough sympathy from relatives and friends not to desperately need your doctor's. But if you're not getting support anywhere else and you feel too intimidated by your doctor to ask for help, or if he or she doesn't seem capable of offering anything not obtainable by prescription, it's time to start looking for a more compatible doctor.

Home Remedies.

Anyone who's lived through colic (and, according to the statistics, about a fifth of all parents have) has emerged with an arsenal of tricks that worked at least once or twice. The following list is offered because we all want to do everything we can to comfort babies who so clearly hurt. But it's also important to realize that sometimes nothing works, and you're not a bad parent for simply letting him cry and getting through the best you can.

- *Burping/Massaging.* Colicky babies often seem especially gassy. Research indicates that while they don't have *more* gas than noncolicky babies, they may have more trouble passing it. It can't hurt to be extremely diligent about burping after feedings. You can also gently massage the baby's stomach with your hands. Or try laying the baby on her back and gently kneading her legs up against her stomach and chest. After a few minutes, this seems to push gas out one end or the other.

- *Keeping the Baby Vertical.* At least one researcher postulated that lying down (especially on her back) may make it more difficult for the baby to pass gas. In this case, holding the baby over your shoulder, in a front-pack, or in an infant seat may provide relief.

- *Motion/Warmth.* Carrying the baby against your body in a Snugli carrier or some other carrier during the day provides the same sense of comfort. But since you can't do that *all* day, you may be able to get some help from technology. Windup swings lull many babies to sleep; so do car rides. Mothers have said their infants also seemed comforted by the sounds of the vacuum cleaner, or by lying (supervised, of course) on top of a functioning clothes washer or dryer. Sometimes a warm water bottle (make sure it's warm on the inside of your wrist, not hot) is also comforting.

- *Sucking.* This seems to relax most babies completely, so if you're nursing a colicky baby, it's only a matter of time until you begin to feel like a human pacifier. There's probably nothing wrong with that, except eventually either your patience or the skin on your nipples will begin to wear thin. If he won't accept the first rubber pacifier you try, he may take another brand that's shaped differently. Unfortunately, some babies just don't seem interested in substitutes.

• *Visual Distraction.* Very young infants seem to be fascinated by stark visual contrasts—enough, sometimes, to be distracted from their crying. If you have bold modern prints with bright colors, dark outlines, or bold borders hanging in your home, try taking the baby on a little art-appreciation tour. You may be surprised at how long she seems mesmerized. You can also buy one-dimensional black-and-white toys, take modern art books from the library, or take her on a field trip to a museum.

• *Sleeping Together.* There are a lot of other issues tied up with whether you want to have an infant in bed with you all night, but many exhausted parents cite night-long colic as a good reason to give it a try. You don't live long with colic without having the agonizing experience of lulling the baby to sleep on your chest or shoulder, only to have him startle awake, screaming, the moment you try to put him in his own bed. Many babies seem to appreciate the warmth and comfort of their parents' bodies, and to sleep better in contact with them. You may not sleep so well with a baby in your bed—but you may get even less sleep pacing the floors all night.

Staying Sane.

Your baby will survive colic and will flourish. The question is, what shape will *you* be in by then? Every first baby creates some pressure on the new mother's relationships, work, and self-image. But a colicky baby intensifies those pressures, shrinks the rewards (at least, for the first few months), and isolates the new mother in ways that make it even harder to cope.

Well-wishers will assault you with their hearty congratulations, never suspecting what life with the little "bundle of joy" is actually like. Other new mothers may eye you with horror if you confess how strung out you feel; their babies, while demanding, don't strain the family's emotional, mental, and physical resources to bankruptcy. In the effort to keep from taking out your inevitable anger and frustration on the baby, you may find yourself turning it on the people around you: your husband, who agreed that a baby would be such a fine idea; your doctor, who can't "fix" it; your old friends who always understood everything else but don't get this at all.

■ *Take the Alcoholics Anonymous Approach.* You know, "one day at a time." Three months seems like a long, long time to you now. So just concentrate on making it through every day as well as you can.

■ *Take Any Help You Can Get.* And if people don't offer, ask them. People who haven't been through colic don't really understand what it's like, and they probably don't realize how badly you need some relief.

■ *Take the Baby Out.* It's easy to be deterred from outings with a colicky baby by the fear that the baby will make a huge scene in public. Obviously, you should keep a screaming infant out of movie theaters, concert halls, libraries, and fine restaurants. But there are lots of places it really doesn't matter if the baby cries: on a country road, on a city street, on a beach, in a shopping mall. You'll feel like you got aired out. And the process of getting her there and back, in the front-pack, car, or carriage, is likely to lull her to sleep.

■ *Get Out without the Baby.* Even if you don't have easy access to relatives or hired sitters, there are ways of getting an hour to yourself now and then. After one of those days when you've almost hurled the baby at your husband as he walked in the door, the best relaxant may be to go out for a walk or a jog. Even an expedition to the supermarket—*alone*—can seem tremendously liberating. You might want to guarantee yourself a regular night out by registering for some ongoing class or activity.

Getting out with your husband (without the baby) is also a good idea. If you don't want to make a whole evening of it, the baby will survive perfectly well for two hours while you grab hamburgers. The sitter will survive perfectly well, too, and two hours of peace will make more of an impact on your life than two hours of screaming will make on the sitter's (unless the sitter is pregnant with her first child).

■ *Go Back to Work.* If you've been debating the timing of your return to work, a colicky child might be a good reason to go back early—especially if you're working part-time. This guarantees you regular time away from the baby and also reminds you that colic will not be a permanent part of your life.

■ *Baby Yourself.* Take whatever chance you get to do something nice for yourself, whether that means an hour of television in the morning, a nap in the afternoon, a glass of wine before dinner, a bath in the evening, or all of the above. The baby won't thank you for the incredibly hard work you're doing, so you have to thank yourself.

■ *Read.* The best book currently in print on the subject of why some babies cry so much and what (if anything) you can do about it is Sheila Kitzinger's *The Crying Baby* (Penguin, 1990). There are two others that have gone out of print but may still be found in libraries or second-hand bookshops: *Crybabies—Coping with Colic: What to Do When Baby Won't Stop Crying* by Dr. Marc Weissbluth, a pediatrician and father, and *Infant Colic: What It Is and What You Can Do About It* by Christopher Farran, a medical writer and also a father. The "facts" in these three books sometimes contradict one another; still, you may derive comfort from their descriptions of other parents' experiences.

■ *And Above All . . .* Remember that it's perfectly okay to feel at times as though you hate or resent the baby—as long as you don't do anything to hurt the baby. Many perfectly nice, decent,

gentle women come through a brush with colic saying they understand for the first time why some mothers abuse their children.

If you do ever feel you might hurt the baby, call someone
immediately—your mother, your husband, your pediatrician or
obstetrician, or a child-abuse hotline.

Otherwise, trust that once the colic diminishes, and especially
once the baby begins smiling and interacting with you, you'll
remember what you thought motherhood was supposed to be all
about.

Old Wives' Tales

"It's Very Hard Not to Take It Personally."

Starting around the second week, when I tried to nurse her at
night, she'd start screaming and trying to climb up my chest. Or
it might start spontaneously around 3:30 and go on till around
6:00 A.M.

When I took her to the doctor, he said she was physically okay
and it was probably colic. But they told me to give her only soy
formula and to stay away from dairy products myself because she
might have a lactose intolerance. So I did that for about six weeks
and then, when she was about eight weeks old, I just stopped
nursing, because I felt like I couldn't eat anything anymore. But I
hadn't noticed any real difference in her. She was still screaming.

I can remember feeling like I just hated her. Once I just picked
her up and starting shaking her, and it was a few moments before
I realized it was a *baby* I was shaking. It's very hard not to take it
personally.

I found myself calling my husband at the office and saying,
"She's screaming, and I can't stand it anymore. Could you please
just come home and take her!" I found myself resenting her and
resenting my husband for convincing me to have her. I resented
the fact I hadn't done this ten years earlier, when I might have
had more energy to deal with it.

I resented everyone. Because you realize that no one else really gives a damn about you. They say politely, "Oh, really, she's colicky?" But they don't understand what you're living with every day. Even my mother. I'd tell her about it, and she'd say, "Oh, the poor baby!" And I'd think, "Mom, what about poor *me!*"

But it made me feel better to have it diagnosed as colic, because at least I knew it wasn't something I was doing wrong. And then I found a way to deal with her. She hated to be rocked or cradled in my arms. She liked to be held against my shoulder and walked, and I would sort of bounce her up and down and make a low, humming noise. And sometimes I would wrap a small hot water bottle up and put it between her stomach and my chest.

Around fourteen weeks, it tapered off. Instead of having a bad time after every feeding, she'd just cry from 3:00 to 6:00 P.M. And then that stopped, too.

"We Were Like Zombies."

In the beginning, for the first week or two, she seemed to sleep most of the time. Then, when she started waking more, she did it at night. She had day and night completely reversed. She'd cry for eight or nine hours at a stretch.

My milk supply hadn't really established itself yet, but the only thing that seemed to help the crying was nursing. Sometimes there didn't seem to be anything there, and she would howl, from disappointment, I assume. People started telling me, "She's not getting enough to eat. Give her formula." But other people had told me that would happen, that people would say those things, and I should just hang on, so I did.

We were up for nights on end. The cry was so piercing that neither of us could sleep. We put the whole rest of our lives on hold, because we were like zombies. I was sore all the time from carrying her around in weird positions.

We were trying to do what the books said, to be calming. Neither of us ever lost our temper—at her. But we did yell at each other. We blamed each other, I think, because we were both

scared out of our minds. But neither of us could admit our inse-
curities. One of us would say, "You're doing that wrong. You made
her cry." Eventually I realized we were reassuring ourselves of our
fitness to parent by accusing the other and seeing what the other
would say in defense, and see if it was a good defense so that we
should adopt that behavior, too.

We were constantly saying, "She's crying because she's too
hot." "No. She's crying because she's too cold." And he would
say, over and over, "Feed her; she's hungry." And I'd say, "I just
fed her for two hours. How can you say she's hungry?" And he'd
keep insisting.

So finally, in desperation, I'd give her the breast again, and the
worst thing was, she *would* nurse. She was insatiable.

At one point, I got so concerned about how much she was
nursing that I called the lactation expert at the hospital and
asked if she was normal. The expert said, "Would you say that
her nursing time totals more than twelve solid hours a day?" I
thought about it, and figured it could be as much as eight. But she
wasn't impressed. She said as long as it was under twelve, it was
normal.

The two things that worked best for us were letting her sleep
with us and being very careful to burp her, no matter how long it
took. When we put her in the crib, for whatever reason, she'd
wake up immediately, crying. But when she sleeps with us, she
seems to wake up, look around to see we're there, and then go
back to sleep.

We never did find out what was bothering her. The crying just
gradually began to get better after about a month. At first, we
didn't even notice it was happening.

Also, it took us three months to figure out that, sometimes,
when she makes that high, piercing cry, we can put her down and
within three minutes she's asleep. We thought every cry had to be
stopped. It didn't occur to us that what in an adult would sound
like total, inconsolable anguish might, in an infant, not have
much emotional significance. Sometimes it just seems that that's
what she needs to do to find her way to sleep.

Recommended Reading

On the baby's development from month to month:

The First Twelve Months of Life: Your Baby's Growth From Month to Month by Frank Caplan and Theresa Caplan, The Princeton Center for Infancy and Early Childhood. Bantam, New York, 1995.
Infants and Mothers: Differences in Development by T. Berry Brazelton, M.D. Delacorte, New York, 1989.

On colic:

Crybabies: Coping with Colic—What to Do When Baby Won't Stop Crying by Marc Weissbluth, M.D. Arbor House, New York, 1984.
The Crying Baby by Sheila Kitzinger. Penguin, New York, 1990.
Infant Colic: What It Is and What You Can Do About It by Christopher Farran. Scribners, New York, 1983.

eight

Ideal *Having a baby cements the bond between husband and wife.*

Fact *A new baby may severely test even a close marriage.*

I t's easy, today, to have an equal, androgynous marriage before (or without) children. The husband works; the wife works. Both contribute funds for household expenses and can afford a few gadgets and baubles at whim. When he travels, she relishes the evenings of solitude and curls up with a junky book and a pint of ice cream. When she works late, he takes in a tacky horror flick with a buddy. They work out some system for the household chores, and it's no big deal; both of them spend most of their waking hours elsewhere.

Enter the infant. Suddenly, he's "working" and she's "not working," even though she's putting in a 168-hour week at home. Money's tighter: She's stopped bringing in a paycheck or if she hasn't, spends most of it on the baby-sitter. When he travels, she panics at being left alone for days on end with total responsibility and no backup. There are more household chores and less time to get them done, and he doesn't seem to realize they need doing at all.

Most couples expect joy and happiness from the birth of a new baby—not added stress. There's no way to predict how much stress a baby will add to your relationship; it depends on what the relationship was like to start with, as well as on what the baby is like (colicky or sweetly sleepy), how both of you earn a living (on the fast track or on flextime), and how much help and support you have (extended families, sitters, cleaning people).

Nevertheless, when women talk about their post-baby marriages, a number of issues seem to come up over and over, most of them centering on role conflict—confusion or disagreement over duties or responsibilities.

Over the past fifteen years, the barriers between men and women—between the roles of Mommy and Daddy on the one hand and Mr. and Ms. Junior Executive on the other—are supposed to have broken down, so that men feel as comfortable changing diapers as women do demanding raises.

But it's certainly possible that the women's movement moved an army of editors and producers more profoundly than it did the average American male, for while children's books, women's magazines, movies, and sitcoms now offer an amazing number of Superwoman and Househusband role models, an amazing number of real husbands would still rather do almost anything on earth they can possibly think of than voluntarily, on their own initiative, without first hanging around for half an hour pretending not to notice the smell, change a diaper.

The issue, though, isn't necessarily how fast or how happily your husband changes diapers; it's how fast and how happily you *expect* him to do it. You may be perfectly happy with a husband who never gives a bottle, never gets up in the middle of the night, and never gives you an evening out to yourself—if you believe he's doing his job and you're doing yours.

That's not to say that any problems are all in your own mind. Few people completely accept that strict, traditional division of labor anymore. Unfortunately, no one has developed a universally fair and applicable design to replace it. So in the post-feminist marriage, all roles are constantly under negotiation. A smaller share of the child-care burden may permit you more freedom to fulfill your own needs, but you may end up with all sorts of guilt, resentment, and arguing over who's getting how much freedom and who's taking how much responsibility.

In other words, you're less likely to run into marital problems if you and your husband completely agree on how much parenting and how much wage earning each of you should do—regardless of the respective amounts. And you can't necessarily predict this agreement before the baby is born. Many a woman who expected to be completely fulfilled by motherhood has found herself resenting the husband who "gets to" go off to an office, escaping inconsolable cries and uninterrupted isolation. And many a woman who once resolved never to become financially dependent on her husband ends up wondering how he can coldly stand by and watch her "have to" return to work, leaving their baby in the care of strangers.

▪ *Who "Gets to" Work and Who "Has To."* Attitudes toward working have undergone a profound transformation since our parents' generation. The "jobs" they held to support us and give us the best possible start in life are now the "careers" to which we look for personal fulfillment as well as a reliable check. Feminism taught us that we, like men, were entitled to this fulfillment, and that, at the very least, we'd better organize our lives so we could support ourselves if we *had* to.

Those of us who grew up with or since feminism have inherited a confused jumble of expectations: We now know that careers are composed of jobs, which often seem dull, trivial, infuriating, and stifling—and still pay less than men's. Yet we also know we can't just give up to the (supposed) domestic bliss of pre–Betty Friedan suburbia, because the dangers have been too highly publicized. Who'll take care of our children if we don't? But who'll take care of us if our husbands walk out and our resumés are rusty? Wanting to "have it all" isn't simply a bourgeois woman's selfish fantasy, it's a theory of self-defense.

Having a child forces you to sort out all your feelings on these issues, with results that may surprise you. It's not simply that

"having it all" has a painfully high price; giving up any part of it
may also have a high price.

Before we had the baby, we expected to split the responsibility equally, or as equally as we could, considering that he
was going to keep working full-time and I'd do something
part-time or free-lance that I hadn't decided on yet. I'd had
enough office jobs to have gotten pretty disgusted by all the
politicking and the ladder climbing.

It was a shock to me how abandoned I felt when he walked
out the door every morning. He was going back to his nice, stable job, while my whole future as a working person suddenly
seemed in doubt. He was going to his nice, quiet office, while I
was walking around the living room for hours on end, trying to
calm a screaming infant. He got dressed up like a grown-up; he
talked to other grown-ups; he got to go to coffee shops for lunch.
I even envied his hour each way on the train, because at least
he got to read the paper, which is more than I did for months.

I saved enough money so that I could take a year off after
the baby was born. I've worked my whole life, and I certainly
didn't expect going back to be emotionally difficult. But when
she was around six months old and I realized it was time to start
updating my resumé, I found I didn't want to do it. You get
very close to your own baby, and it's hard to imagine that
anyone else could give her as much as her own parents.

But I have to go back, because we can't live on my husband's income alone. I feel a lot of anger and resentment
toward him about it, even though I know it's stupid and illog-
ical. He's self-employed, and he works a lot of hours, but he
doesn't make much money. And what he does is a social service, and I wouldn't want him to have to do the kind of thing
he'd have to do to make more.

I took a three-month maternity leave and then went back
to work part-time a few weeks ago. And actually, there's been
more conflict over changing roles since I went back than there

was when I was home full-time. At least then I seemed to have time to accomplish everything I wanted to get done.

Finally, the other day, we had a discussion about it. I told him I didn't think his life had changed that much since the baby was born. He got pretty defensive and said his thinking had changed a lot. And I said, "I understand that it's changed in some ways. But in fact you still get up and go to work whenever you want, you come home whenever you're done, and even though you may think you're trying to get done earlier than you used to, most nights you're still not back till seven-thirty or eight. And if you decide you're going to go in to work on a weekend, it doesn't occur to you that maybe that will upset me because I need to have two hours to myself on a Saturday afternoon."

So finally he agreed that he would have to be a lot more sensitive about these things, especially on the days I work and generally feel overwhelmed.

I'm enjoying working at home, and I'm enjoying my time with the baby. I don't envy my husband at all; in fact, I feel sorry for him. He's involved in an institutional structure that matters to him not at all. He could get all his work done in four hours a day, but, working in a major corporation, he has all sorts of meetings and social distractions. Everyone goes to the cafeteria together for morning coffee; that's forty-five minutes out of your workday, even before you get to lunch. Of course, they talk about work-related issues. But they also waste a lot of time talking about what was on TV last night and where Sally's taking her vacation.

It helps that he's the kind of person he is. He doesn't come home at night and say, "Dear, I've had a very hard day, could you fix me a martini?" In fact, a few days ago, he said, "I just had the hardest day I've had in months. Where's that baby?"

■ *Who's "in Charge" at Home and Who "Helps Out."*   The flip side of the question of who's earning money and building a career is the question of who's taking care of what on the home front.

Probably, you're doing most of it, whether you've got an outside job or not.

As with wage-earning work, those of us who grew up with the women's movement have accumulated lots of mismatched notions about housework. Feminism convinced us that it wasn't as fulfilling or respectable as paid work. But life presents us with the indisputable evidence that it still needs to get done. Husbands, on the other hand, tend almost universally to overlook that fact, leaving us three unpleasant options:

1. Nag.
2. Do it yourself.
3. Both of the above.

The division of housework? It's not fair, and it never has been fair, and it never will be fair. Even with the baby, and with me working part-time, my husband still expects me to cook his dinner, make his lunch, do the laundry, and go grocery shopping. That's just the way it is, and I have to accept it. But we need to discuss it frequently in order for him to realize how much I'm doing. We need to keep the lines of communication open, and unfortunately sometimes we don't do that and it builds up and then we have a big fight.

We have cleaning people come in, and that gets some of the bigger housework issues out of the way. But even when we both worked full-time, I was always the one with domestic issues on my mind. He'd never sit in the car on the way home and worry about what we were having for dinner that night, which I would. Occasionally, in the first few weeks with the baby, that was a problem. He'd walk in at 7:30 P.M. on a day when she'd been screaming for hours and say, "So, what's for dinner?" Fortunately, he never had the insensitivity to follow up with, "But you've been home all day!"

At some level, I'd love to have a husband who was interested in being home a day or two a week, but my husband is just not that kind of person. Sometimes I get frustrated and resentful because he doesn't seem to understand how much I'm really doing. It would be wonderful if he'd remember to take the garbage out without my saying anything, because then I feel like I'm nagging. Once I say something, he'll do it, and the general pattern is that he's good for a couple of weeks and then gets overwhelmed and forgets. So it comes up again and again.

- *He's No Good with the Baby.*   Some men feel completely overwhelmed by newborn babies, who can't yet be sociable or play games. They are immensely relieved when their wives assume complete responsibility for the baby's care, and readily admit that they aren't as "good" with the infant as she is.

Of course, there are many women who are completely freaked out by newborn babies. They're afraid of under- or over-feeding them, dropping them during a bath, or not recognizing the symptoms of dire illnesses.

The difference is that in most cases the woman is forced to take responsibility for the infant whether she feels comfortable or not. Gradually, as she sees herself doing okay, she does feel comfortable. But she may find she can't get occasional time off because her husband can't be trusted to do a good job. And he's never learned to do a good job because neither of them ever trusted him with the responsibility.

If this sounds familiar, you might want to think about getting out of the house every once in a while, leaving your husband as baby-sitter. (Trying to take your break in another room isn't the same, as you've probably discovered. It leaves you too vulnerable to endless questions about when the baby last ate, when the last diaper change occurred, what *you* usually do with her around this time every day. . . .)

And if that doesn't work, try to hold on. Lots of men are more willing to spend time with their babies as the babies become more interesting, as they begin to smile and crawl, walk and talk.

For the first few weeks after the baby was born, I really thought my husband didn't like him very much. It really scared me. I thought, "He hates him, and I've ruined his life, so now he's probably going to leave us."

But Bob thought the baby didn't like him either. He was with me all day, and I fed him and changed his diapers, so of course he got used to me. But there was a period where, when Bob came home at night, the baby would start fussing and crying, and Bob really took it personally.

It surprised me. Anyone who'd met him before would have thought he'd be the perfect father. He loves kids. I think part of the problem was that I had the chance, in the hospital, to spend a lot of time with the baby. I was just thrown into the middle of the situation, and I had to handle it. And by the time we came home, I already seemed to know what I was doing. But he didn't know how to stop him from crying. He didn't really know when he needed changing. It seemed to him like a lot of responsibility he just couldn't handle.

But that seems to have passed. Once the baby started smiling at Bob, I think he really started feeling like he was dealing with a person. Now, I sometimes get the feeling that the baby likes him more than he likes me.

When I was pregnant, I used to tease my husband that from the moment he came home from work to the moment she went to bed the baby was going to be his responsibility, because I was quitting my job to care for her full-time all day. Well, as it turned out, for the time when I nursed that was somewhat unrealistic. But for the most part, I'm happy with the amount he's doing.

But the other day, I was just exhausted. I'd been with her all day, and I'd done a lot of housework and even made cookies. And I really didn't feel like holding her and giving her a bottle, so I asked if he would do it.

She drank about half the bottle, and then she was just lying there contentedly in his lap. And he said, "I think Terry wants you." I said I'd been with her all day. He said, "And I've been working all day." And I said, "So have I." But then I said that if he really didn't want to hold her, he could give her to me. Which he did.

The next night, she was real fussy when he got home. He said, "All day long I've been looking forward to playing with her, and now she's fussy." So I said, "Well, she spends more time with me than she does with you. Maybe she's going through a stage of development where she'd prefer to be with me because she sees me more." He asked what he could do about it, and I suggested that he spend more time with her. "I do spend time with her," he said.

Well, maybe it wasn't totally nice of me, but I said, "What about last night? There was a perfect opportunity, and you chose not to hold her. When I'm alone with her during the day, there's no one else to turn to, so I have to hold her all the time, and give her bottles, and change her diapers. If you want her to feel as close to you as she does to me, then when you're home you have to spend time with her. That's natural."

And I think now he does make more of an effort.

At the beginning, I was completely responsible for everything: the house, the meals, Katie. There were times when the only way I could get him to pay attention to her was to put her in his lap. He never volunteered to take care of her. I'd tell him, "Just once, I'd like to hear you ask to take her out somewhere, and really mean it. I might not even take you up on the offer. I'd just like you to ask."

Finally, one night I just said good-bye and walked out for about forty minutes. I thought it was the only way he was ever going to learn to have any contact with her.

Eventually, he did take her out. The first time, he took her to a mall, and she came back with a black eye. "Your worst fears have come true," he said. She'd fallen into a box in an aisle in a discount store.

It's much better now than it was in the first few months. It just seemed to take him a long time to acknowledge her. I think it happened at around three months. By that point, I was used to nursing, and I was losing some weight and getting over the New Mommy stuff. And I think he was over his fear a little more and felt she was more interactive.

But she's fifteen months old now, and he's just given her a bath for the first time. And that's only because I accused him of not having any idea how to do it and dared him to try.

- *Jealousy over the Baby—and Each Other.* A baby's appetites are voracious, and it may sometimes feel as though he's absorbing everything both parents have the energy to produce—milk, money, and love. Embedded in your husband's inability to deal with the baby may be jealousy over the way the close relationship between mother and child might seem to exclude him. You'd probably feel the same sort of jealousy toward him if he were with the baby as much as you, and you may in fact feel it for the baby's care giver if you return to a full-time job.

The jealousy may go both ways. Perhaps, before you had a child, you babied each other. Now, all three of you compete for that attention, and the baby always wins. You resent your husband for still expecting to be taken care of, when he can damn well take care of himself and you clearly have so many other responsibilities. At the same time, you also resent him because he doesn't seem to notice that *you* can use a bit of babying yourself.

In the first few weeks when I was home all day with the baby, my husband would get back from work and I'd want his total undivided attention and he'd want to play with the baby. I was almost jealous of the attention he was giving her. I felt like, "Yes, she's a wonderful kid, but I've been with her all day long and I need someone to just be with *me* for a while, to talk to me and hug me."

My marriage is definitely rockier than it was before the baby. I don't think it's going to be permanent, but the fact she's had some serious medical problems has been a strain on both of us. And a lot of it is that we just don't seem to have time anymore. I used to be babied by my husband, but now he just doesn't have time. He always gave me backrubs, but I've only had two in the last three months.

When my husband used to travel on business, he'd call home at night and say how much he missed me. Now he calls and says, "I miss Sarah so much," and I say, "A-hem!" and he says, "Oh, and of course I miss you, too."

■ *"Lightning Rods in a Storm."* It's possible that a certain amount of the resentment building up between you and your husband is completely irrational, that it isn't caused by any fundamental problem in your relationship, but by the accumulated pressures of all the other stress in your lives which have no other outlet. In particular, it's tempting (and perhaps safer) to take out frustration with the baby on your husband, who isn't completely defenseless.

It wasn't till much later that I realized how great a toll the colic had taken on my marriage. We were both so scared and irritated and overwhelmed by the constant crying, but we knew it wasn't her fault and we didn't want to take it out on her. So we took it out on one another. We were like lighting rods in a storm, trying to guide all this destructive energy to earth safely, without destroying anything.

I had always felt about my marriage that we were so in love that if one of us were ever asked, "Would you give up your life to save your spouse?" we would both unhesitatingly answer "Yes." But, to mix my metaphors, we were like two drowning people, each of us expecting the other to save him without being aware that the other one was drowning, too. I was too exhausted to care about his needs and he was too exhausted to care about mine.

■ *"What Happened to Our Sex Life?"* Although post-baby sex may be every bit as satisfying as pre-baby sex, you're almost certain to have less of it—for months, if not years, to come. An extremely unscientific sample of women interviewed for this book showed that if a couple had been having sex twice a week before the baby, they might manage once every ten days or so afterwards. The only woman who claimed her sex life hadn't diminished since her baby's birth said she and her husband had normally had sex once a month.

Most women, and many men, don't seem to feel much desire for a long time after the birth of a new baby. In the woman's case, there are some obvious physical reasons, including the vaginal dryness caused by nursing and the healing of episiotomy or cesarean scars. If you haven't lost all the pregnancy weight, you may not feel so attractive. If you had a traumatic childbirth, you may worry about getting pregnant again. Your almost continual physical contact with the baby may satisfy your need to cuddle. When the baby's not with you, you may still find your mind is tuned to the twenty-four-hour Mommy channel, waiting for the next peep. And by the end of the day, you and your husband may find yourselves simply too exhausted to think about sex.

A diminished sex life in itself won't hurt your marriage. But if your marriage is having other troubles accommodating the baby— if you're fighting a lot more than you did before—then you may end up with a chicken-and-egg situation: You're having less sex because you're so mad at each other, and in turn you're losing the chance for the sort of nonverbal healing that the intimacy of sex encourages.

> Our sex life is definitely not what it was. For one thing, I was on the pill before, and now I'm using a diaphragm, which I hate. I don't feel comfortable incorporating it into our sex life, and I'm still getting used to how it works, so it's definitely an interruption. As for quantity, it's definitely decreased. But it's not like there are a lot of nights when I'm wishing and nothing's happening. I think we both feel the same way about it, which is tired.

> I want my sex life back. For years, before we got married, if we didn't have sex at least once a day it was really unusual.

And now we might get to it once a week. It seems like a good night when we just *talk* about having sex. We're just exhausted, and I have very little desire, I think, because of the breast-feeding. I'm really dry. Even when I feel aroused, there's no indication. And sex shouldn't be a chore.

We recently filled out a survey in one of those parenting magazines, and one of the questions was, "If you had an extra hour each day, what would you do?" The options were something like: read or watch TV, sleep, make love, or pursue your hobby. And both of us marked "sleep."

How do you have a normal sex life when you're always pissed at your husband because he hasn't taken care of the babies enough, or he's pissed at you because you haven't? Since the babies were born, we might have sex once a month. I remember once we did it twice in a week and I thought, "Wow, that's a lot!" Very rarely do desire and circumstance coincide.

I'm a little embarrassed that I'm not more upset about it. The babies mean so much to me, and I know that's one of the things that's getting in the way of my relationship with my husband. I just have much less need for the cuddling part of sex. Actually, I also have much less need for the sexy part of sex. I'm sure, because I also have no desire to masturbate.

But it doesn't bother me that much. Actually, I think the thing that bothers me more is how little it bothers me.

Recommended Reading

For Better, For Worse: A Candid Chronicle of Five Couples Adjusting to Parenthood by Susan Squire. Bantam, New York, 1994.

The Second Shift: Working Parents and the Revolution at Home by Arlie Hochschild with Anne Machung. Avon, New York, 1990.

The Transition to Parenthood: How a Child Changes a Marriage, Why Some Couples Grow Closer and Others Apart by Jay Belsky, Ph.D., and John Kelly. Dell, New York, 1995.

War and Peace: Four Marital Survival Skills

1. *Diplomatic Talks.* It's possible that any domestic problems you may be having are the result of a failure to communicate. In other words, he doesn't *know* how overwhelmed you feel, because he's too wrapped up in his own problems. He doesn't *know* how much energy the baby absorbs, or how often the kitchen floor gets washed, or how depressing it is to go whole days without talking to other grown-ups, because he doesn't do any of these things and you haven't talked about it or asked clearly for help.

The solution, in the best of all possible worlds, is to bring it up in a nonthreatening manner at a time when you are not feeling angry. The two of you sit down and calmly discuss how he could help you relieve your household responsibilities and give you a few hours a week to yourself.

2. *Laying Siege.* Sometimes being a mature adult doesn't work. Sometimes you talk and he goes selectively deaf. Perhaps he thinks you're just letting off steam and not really expecting a change of behavior on his part. In this case, you might want to talk louder and more frequently, especially at moments when he has just taken advantage of you and you are really pissed off. This tactic is also known as Having a Big Fight and is sometimes more effective for getting your point across than calm, reasonable discussion.

3. *Guerrilla Warfare.* At a certain point, the only effective strategy is to walk out for a day or a few hours, leaving him in charge of baby and home. Whether you're trying to get him to develop daddying skills or simply to appreciate how hard you work, there's no substitute for firsthand experience.

4. *La Résistance.* If your problem isn't one of communication but of basic disagreement over roles, you may have to just swallow the unfairness of the situation if you want to preserve the marriage. This doesn't mean surrendering the rest of your life to child rearing. A time will come when the baby will start sleeping through the night, will play with a coloring book for an hour at a time without your active supervision, will eventually go to school. In the meantime, you have assumed an enormous responsibility, and though that isn't much praised these days, it's still a very noble act.

Old Wives' Tales

"Why Is a Husband Doing a Wife a Favor when He's Changing His Own Baby's Diapers?"

Dora, thirty, was a working-class mother of an eight-month-old boy named Sean. After agonizing over the decision, she quit her job to stay home with him full-time. Her husband, Mike, seemed upset by the baby, and she was upset by his attitude. But both were avoiding a confrontation.

Mike loses patience with the baby really fast, and it really aggravates me. It really gets me mad. He doesn't seem to understand that the baby cries to communicate, because he's hungry or tired, and not to annoy Mike. He gets angry, and I don't think that's an appropriate response.

And he's not doing as much as I expected. In the beginning he was fine, but then he trailed off. He seems to expect that I'll do everything for the baby, even when he's home, because he goes out and works. We talked about arranging everything fairly before I quit work myself, and I was very happy about it. But in reality, it just hasn't come out that way. If I ask him to watch the baby, I have to remind him to change the baby. It wouldn't occur to him that that might be *part* of watching the baby.

When he does do it, he acts like he's doing me a favor. But why is a husband doing his wife a favor when he's changing his own baby's diapers?

I think about it a lot. I'm never sure if the problem is in my own mind, if I have the right to feel the way I do. I wonder if I should be making more allowances for the fact that he works such long hours. And sometimes I think that if I were more of a Supermom or a Superwife, Sean wouldn't make so much noise, and Mike could come home and relax.

I try not to spring it on Mike, but you know how, when you're down, it seems like you'll just come out and say everything you've been thinking about, in a nasty way instead of a positive way. He's a quiet person, so it's hard to get him to talk about it. I've been trying to hint at things, to say them in a nice way at a nice time. But there have been times when I've just exploded.

The thing is, I just expect him to *see* sometimes that I need help, and it seems that he's blind. I try to give him leeway. I know he's tired. But there are times when I just need help and I can't disguise it anymore. I just need someone to take the baby away from me for an hour. He should just *offer* to do it, so I don't have to hint, hint, hint around.

It definitely seems that our marriage isn't as good as it was before the baby came. We don't seem very close anymore, and I think he resents the baby because of that. He feels the baby has come between us. And I don't think that's true. I think he's letting the baby come between us, that he's *making* it an obstacle.

I know he's upset, because he shows it in little ways. But he won't come out and discuss it. Maybe it would help him to talk to other fathers. But I don't know how to help him, and I get mad because I think, "You're just going to have to do this yourself." Before the baby, if he was mad about something, I'd try to jolly it out of him. But now I don't have time to play those games. I feel like, "If you have something to say, just say it. I don't have time to go around in circles with, 'What's wrong, honey?' 'Nothing.'"

In some of the mothers' groups I've joined, I've brought this up in a roundabout way. But people don't seem to want to talk about it. I've heard other women make references to similar problems. It seems like they're almost bursting to talk about it, but they're embarrassed. Like it's somehow their fault. Or maybe they shouldn't be feeling these things, that they don't have a right to feel that way about their husbands.

But I know I need a break. At the end of the day, it would be so nice just to go and take a bath and not have to worry about the baby for a second. But it seems like, even when I do leave him with the baby for a minute, I can't trust him. Something always happens and the baby starts crying. And he gets aggravated, and that makes it worse. So I can't get a break.

I'd be better off leaving that baby with a sitter than with my own husband.

"I Hardly Ever Feel That Surge of Love I Used to Feel for Him."

Faith is a twenty-eight-year-old graphic designer whose baby, Jon, was four months old at the time of the interview. Like Dora, she was surprised at how uncomfortable her husband seemed to be around the baby, and disappointed that he didn't take more responsibility at home. Her part-time work made her less dependent on him emotionally but didn't solve the basic problems in the relationship.

Harry and I have always had slight communication problems. You know how you're not supposed to hurt the other person or be nasty or cut the other person down? Well, we do that, and we've done it since before the baby. So we didn't start out as well as some other couples.

I've never felt that he does enough around the house, so I've always nagged him. He's one of those males who got spoiled by his mother and isn't used to cleaning up after himself. He's never done the 50 percent I think he should do. Of course, if you called him on it, I'm sure he'd agree that it's fair for him to do 50 percent. But he perceives that he does more than he actually does, because he doesn't understand how much more there is to do.

I thought he'd be great with the baby. Our best friends have a baby, and the father is great about child care. When he was out of a job, he stayed home and took care of the child while the mother worked. He really takes the responsibility for their everyday life. Harry really wanted to be like that. We were both looking forward to it.

But he's not like that at all. I have to tell him to change diapers. I have to tell him Jon needs a bath. I have to tell him when Jon needs to eat. It doesn't seem to be part of Harry's makeup just to think about these things. He would never just think to change the bathroom towels after they've been hanging up there for a week. I'm the one who thinks about those things.

Also, he goes to a martial arts class three nights a week. In the beginning, when I was home alone all day for three months, I would be dying for him to come home from work. And when he finally came home—sometimes late—I'd give him dirty looks. I don't think he understood how hard it was for me to be alone all day with the baby and all that responsibility, and have him come home for an hour and then leave.

So we established that two nights a week he would take care of the baby. But even so, he doesn't really take the responsibility. I'm the one that says, "Here, honey, can you hold him? Can you change his diapers? Can you give him a bath now?" And, in fact, I end up doing a lot of it, because it's just easier. The only way I ever really do get away from it is to leave the house. But I don't want to leave every night, because I never see Harry, either.

We don't fight that much now. For the first three months, we did, but Jon's gotten a lot easier to care for, and I'm working a few days a week. I enjoy taking care of him. I really look forward to when Harry comes home, but it's not so critical, because I'm getting other adult stimulation. I'm constantly on the go, running errands, and the days go by pretty fast. And it's better because it's spring, and we can get out a lot more than we did in the winter.

But in general the relationship doesn't seem as good as it did before I got pregnant. There's no special warmth. We're just so distant. I hardly ever feel that surge of love I used to feel for him, which makes it all worth it. And I don't know how to go about getting it back except spending more time together again. Right now, I resent him and I know he resents me, and we can't seem to get past that to the good stuff that I think is still there, deep down.

"You Have to Let Certain Dreams and Aspirations Go By-the-By While You Nurture the Child."

Eve, thirty-five, was an artist who had put aside both her art and her wage-earning job to stay home with her daughter; on a part-time basis, her job would not have paid much more than a sitter would cost, and with no sitting she had no un-interrupted time in which to be creative. She found herself resenting her husband, Seth, both because of his refusal to do any child care and his ability to continue on with his own work undisturbed.

I think if I had been twenty-five, I might have been willing to let go of my own career. But at thirty-five, I was interested in doing my own thing. I had a clear idea of exactly what I wanted to do with a day when I got up in the morning, and I was used to having that freedom, of being able to do whatever I wanted, whenever I wanted. So when Sally was born, I felt like my arms and legs were chopped off.

Seth isn't interested in caring for her in any way. She's totally my responsibility. And I'm now considered a "nonproductive" part of the relationship, because I'm not earning money. I'm not appreciated. I get the feeling he thinks I sit around and eat chocolates all day.

What he doesn't seem to understand is that, in this house, the most important thing that is happening is the nurturing of this child. Not his new account. Not his promotion. He should be here helping me to nurture this child, and he's not, and that makes me angry.

But I don't want this friction that has come between us to take over. I refuse to have this anger in the house while I'm raising this baby, because it's going to rub off on her. But to keep an even keel, I have to let things slide that I would never, ever have let slide before. Maybe if he were twenty, I'd try to change him. But he's in his mid-forties, and he's not going to change.

But for someone who was very plugged into the women's movement, this is very hard. It's terrible to go from complete freedom to only being able to talk without articles. You know: "Want this? Mommy go!" I think the problem for most women is that after they have a child, they have to grow up. You have to let certain dreams and aspirations go by-the-by while you nurture the child.

That's my job now. And I'm not going to go around feeling sorry for myself because I can't go do what I feel like doing. I get very tired sometimes, but there's a lot of enjoyment in it also, and it gets to be more fun the older and more independent she gets.

Now that she's through the first year, I'm going to start looking for a job. And then things will have to change around here, because it will be necessary. I'm not allowed to sit here and moan and groan for him to do domestic things, because I'm home, and therefore it becomes my job whether I want it or not. But once I go back to the work force, we'll have to share it, because I can't possibly do it all, and I'll be helping us by bringing money in. I don't think it will be that much of a problem, but talk to me in a couple of years.

Anyway, he's going to be very sorry if he continues at this pace. He's very out of touch with her development. He'll say, "Go get the ball," and then be amazed that she does it. But she's actually been doing it for a while.

If I were to find a full-time job, at least half my salary would go to child care. But that's okay with me. It's worth it.

$n^i n_e$

Ideal *Becoming a mother makes you feel so much closer to your own mother.*

Fact *This may be the occasion when your mother—or mother-in-law—finally does drive you nuts.*

The birth of a first child throws you into a new relationship with your parents and your husband's parents—particularly, since you're a woman, with your mother and mother-in-law. Some women say they find themselves suddenly feeling much closer—especially to their mothers. But some find themselves feeling intensely antagonistic—especially toward their mothers-in-law.

Unfortunately, while it's usually assumed to be a time of great joy for all involved, the birth of a baby is often a time of great tension. And unless you have a really splendid, relaxed relationship with your parents and in-laws, you may feel that just coping with the baby's enormous needs is more than you can handle, without having to worry about the grandparents' needs as well.

And the grandparents *are* needy; the newer they are to grandparenting, the needier. A first grandchild means they're still rolling the words "grandmother" or "grandfather" around in their mouths the way you used to roll the word "wife," thinking it was someone much older and more mature than you were. By now their own memories of sleepless nights, tantrums, and endless car rides punctuated by frequent whining "Are-we-there-yet"s have faded. What your baby will stir up from the depths of their memories are the sweet smell of the top of a baby's head, the warm way he snuggles against their bodies, the triumph of being able to make him smile.

■ *Role Model or Rival?*   The baby may also stir up other feelings in your mother and mother-in-law, who are forced at this point to pass the torch of motherhood on to you, ready or not. This means you're going to get advice. You're going to get advice from everyone, of course, but *this* is the advice of that person who did such a good—or terrible—job of raising you or your husband. And this is the advice of someone who really cares whether or not you take it.

My mother always thinks she knows a better way to do everything. I went shopping with her the other day, and she told me that the baby wasn't dressed warmly enough and then that I was patting her too hard when I burped her. One night we all went out to dinner together, and the baby was fussing, and my husband was holding her. And my mother just walked over and grabbed her from him. She stopped crying immediately—you know, sometimes it seems that a new voice will calm her down like that—but I think she really hurt my husband. My sister has a six-year-old, and she's been saying for years that my mother was driving her nuts. Now I know why.

I'm comfortable leaving the baby with my mom, but not with my mother-in-law. She doesn't do things the same way I do. She's very critical, and whenever she's here she makes a comment about something I'm doing or something I'm not doing but ought to be. She says that instead of using an emery board on Judy's fingernails, I should be *biting* them off, because that's what *she* did. And I'm sorry, but that sounds *so* barbaric.

Once, when she got the hiccups, my mother-in-law went and dipped her finger into the sugar jar and stuck her finger in the baby's mouth, and I had a fit. I thought, "How dare you do something like that to my baby without asking me first how I feel about her having sugar!"

She's always been like that, but it used to roll off my back. I guess I don't feel as confident about mothering as I do in other areas of my life.

My mother-in-law had four children, so of course she's an expert. She's always giving me advice. She doesn't like the brand of diaper rash ointment I use. She wants him to wear socks all the time, when I let him go barefoot. She says we hold him too much.

My mother-in-law nursed, but on a schedule. I'm doing it on demand. So she's always telling me I feed him too often. "Maybe you should try to stretch it out to three hours," she says. "You don't have to feed him every time he cries, you know." My mother says some of the same things, but I don't seem to hear it coming from her, or I just say, "No, Ma, we don't do it like that anymore." But with my mother-in-law, I feel really defensive.

I'm so much like my mother that I don't think she'd do things with the baby that I wouldn't want her to. Fortunately, I have a very good relationship with my in-laws, but my mother-in-law can be overwhelming. Then I just tell her, "Mary, don't do that." And she says, "Oh, Clara," and usually goes ahead and does it anyway, and then jokes about how I'm worried.

Actually the worst tension has been between her and my husband. He was much more protective of the baby than I was, probably because I had a tough recovery, and he was doing more of the caretaking in the beginning than I was. They yelled at each other a few times, and finally I took him aside and said I thought he was being a little hard on her. Then I took her aside and said, "I know you raised three beautiful children, but I think that for now you just have to let us run the show here. Marty and I really need to feel confident that we know how to deal with our own child. We need to feel that we know this kid better than anyone else. I know you think I'm crazy, but that's how I am."

And I'm finding that the older Kelly gets, the more willing I am to relinquish her to someone who won't do things exactly my way. There are times when I bite my tongue, but I've also found tactful ways to let them know what she likes, rather than grabbing her back when I think she's upset.

- *Too Close or Too Far Away.* Geography can work for or against you. Nearby grandparents can develop close relationships with their grandchildren, enriching their lives and providing you

---

Advice on Advice: Three Strategies

1. *Deflect it.* This means that, no matter what your actual opinion on the suggestion, you say politely, "That's an interesting idea. I'll certainly think about that." And change the subject.

2. *Counter It.* If you think it's worth arguing over—say, if you're under constant assault on a specific topic, like when to start solid foods or how much a baby should be held—you can start a propaganda war. This means you clip and photocopy any written material supporting your position and bombard your adviser. This strategy worked very well for one woman whose mother kept undermining her breast-feeding (see chapter 4, page 61).

3. *Beg for mercy.* If you're under constant assault by someone who seems to disapprove of everything you do, this is the time to say as gently as you can that you know the suggestions are well intended and may have worked for someone else but that you need to find your own ways of mothering.

---

with crucial overnight baby-sitting. They can also drop by more often than you'd like, with the opportunity to observe firsthand the myriad ways in which you're screwing up as a mother.

Great distances insulate you from scrutiny but also deny grand-parents and children the chance to really get to know one another until the children are old enough to form independent relation-ships. Throughout babyhood, the grandparents fret that the baby will forget them between visits, which the baby does, and every-one feels bad about it. Meanwhile, you are responsible for keeping up the flow of news, snapshots, and—if you can afford it—videotape.

This is the first grandchild on both sides of the family, so as the pregnancy wore on, the excitement reached fever pitch. The nursery would never have been furnished so nicely if it hadn't been for the in-laws pitching in with gifts. But they always seemed to be pushing things on us. They always seemed to be suggesting things a few months ahead of when I naturally would have gotten around to doing them.

As the delivery date drew nearer, my mother-in-law called every single day to find out what was going on. And she'd call right after every doctor's appointment. Finally, two or three days before we had the baby, my husband and I finally said, "Please do not call us every day. You're driving us crazy." We tried to say it as lovingly as possible, but it definitely hurt them a great deal.

Then, in the middle of the really intense part of labor, the nurse called my husband out of the delivery room for a phone call. It was my mother-in-law. She knew we'd gone to the hospital twelve hours before, and she wanted to know what was going on. I remember having a terrible contraction, and really needing my husband to press on my back, and he wasn't there. I'll never forget that she did that. It was a real invasion.

Twenty minutes after the baby was born, my mother-in-law was with us in the recovery room. So much for bonding time. She'd already been at the hospital for an hour.

Then they were at the hospital twice a day. I got home on

a Friday, and they were here all weekend, and every time they came after that they were trying to make an arrangement for the next time they could come, and for who they were going to bring with them. I felt really lucky when finally some of my own family came from out of town, because that was the only reason my in-laws seemed to accept for staying away.

So we had to call them to have a "talk." It was not an easy thing to do. I told them that when something happens to me, I need some time to myself to get used to it. And I thought we needed to fend for ourselves a little bit. I said some other things I'm not too proud of having said, and they said some things, too, and all of this is sort of lingering in the air. People were definitely hurt.

I think we made a little progress. But I just have a different philosophy of family from what they have. They want to be really involved; they have this thing about how families are supposed to be close. I feel like they want to know every time I pass gas. My family is more standoffish, and that's how I feel comfortable. That kind of difference is very hard to overcome.

We've worked out a sort of compromise, where my mother-in-law comes once or twice a week to baby-sit while I go out and have some time to myself. I know they think I'm a cold person who doesn't want to have any family around, but that's not true. I love the fact that this baby will have a relationship with her grandmother. I still think I'm compromising more than they are, but I keep telling myself, at least I'm getting great baby-sitting.

For months after I had the baby, my mother, who lives too far away to visit much, would call three times a week and want to know every single tiny detail about the baby. How much was he sleeping? How much was he eating? Was I sure I had enough milk? How much did he weigh at the last doctor visit? What did the doctor say about weaning? What did the doctor say about solid foods?

It drove me crazy. She was much more anxious about the whole thing than I was, but I felt like every conversation with her planted new doubts in my head that I knew were silly but which I couldn't tune out. Because she was my *mother*.

The other thing that was driving me crazy, although I couldn't admit this until much later, was that she had completely lost interest in me. Before the baby, we used to have these long phone conversations about current events and family gossip and her job and my job. And all of a sudden, at a time when I felt like I had completely lost sight of the person I'd been before diapers and spit-up and breast infections came crashing down on me, all she seemed to want to hear about was diapers and spit-up and breast infections. When I was up nights on end with a screaming baby, she'd say, "Oh, poor baby," not "Oh, poor you." And of course she was never any practical help, because she was too far away.

Eventually, we had a fight about it. She said, "Of course I'm still interested in you," and then for a long time she was really careful to ask me about me before she asked about him. As the baby got older, I guess we also both got more confident that whatever I was doing was okay. Then my brother's wife had a baby, which helped take some of the heat off me. And when I started working again part-time, I wasn't so desperate for reassurance that the old me I remembered from before the baby was still inside.

ten

Ideal *There's so much less social pressure on women today about whether they should stay home or go back to full-time jobs.*

Fact *There's more social pressure than ever, much of it contradictory, so whichever choice you make is bound to include days of self-doubt.*

About twenty-five years ago, if you had decided to go back to your job after having a baby, a lot of people would have thought you were a bad mother—an immature and unfeminine person who couldn't put her child's needs before her own.

These days, a lot of people—particularly your coworkers and old friends who haven't had children of their own yet—will just assume you plan to continue your old work full-time. If you don't, they may think you're a bad Supermother—an immature and old-fashioned person who can't juggle her family's needs with her own desire for self-fulfillment.

And guess what: If you *do* stay on your old job full-time, there will *also* be people (your mother, perhaps, and the mothers in your neighborhood who stay home) who think you're a rotten mother who can't put her children's needs before her own.

So the first rule of thumb for those who are torn between continuing their wage-earning and mothering full-time is that worrying about how others will view your decision won't get you anywhere.

Does that help? Probably not. For by this point, most of us have been exposed to enough material on both sides of the debate to have internalized the dilemma. It won't matter what snide comments actually drip from the lips of interested friends and neighbors; we'll be too busy looking around at other women who've chosen other paths, and wondering if we've done "the right thing."

■ *Mothering through the Ages.* Ironically, all this anxiety and self-doubt is a luxury of modern Western society. As Ann Dally points out in her thoughtful book *Inventing Motherhood,* it's only recently that isolating mothers at home with their young children has been considered an ideal situation.

As Dally argues, until the industrial revolution, most male and female work (except waging war) was done at or very near home. This meant, very simply, that there was no particular conflict between "working" and raising children. Since people tended to live among members of their extended family and perhaps servants, it also meant that mothers had plenty of adult companionship and help, and that children routinely formed significant relationships with grown-ups other than their parents.

Also, the degree of emphasis we place on rearing "happy," well-adjusted children would have seemed absurd to our pre-twentieth-century ancestors. Their priority was survival, and that usually required the whole family to pull together. Each member of the family was expected to serve an economic function. Sons inherited, defended, and if possible augmented their fathers' money. If there was nothing to inherit, they might be sent away at a young age to another household as servants or apprentices. Daughters were expected to marry as their fathers told them to, bringing their husbands dowries, bearing them children, and managing the details of domestic life. In short, society expected obedience, not self-actualization, from children—obedience that would further the parents' ends, not the children's.

The industrial revolution changed all of this. Manufacturing required people to work in factories that were too dangerous for children or in offices where jobs required a level of education children didn't yet have. Wage-earning work suddenly became distinct from family-maintaining work, and doing one began to rule out doing the other.

Even so, for many years, it was still unusual for a mother to spend all her time caring for her own children. If she were well-off, servants would do most of the work for her; if she were poor, her relatives might watch the children while she went out to do a paid job. But as the twentieth century rolled on, families became more mobile, moving away from potentially helpful relatives, and domestic servitude lost its appeal as a career. The modern house-wife, raising 2.6 kids in the splendid isolation of her own home, was born.

But if it took the economic revolution of the nineteenth century to isolate women in their homes, Dally argues, it took the psychological revolution of the twentieth century to enshrine them there. As basic hygienic and medical techniques improved, child-care manuals dropped their initial emphasis on how to keep babies alive and began to grapple with the idea of what constituted a proper moral and intellectual education. Then came Freud, with theories about how childhood trauma might cause lifelong psychological damage. Just at the time mothers were beginning to shoulder the whole child-rearing burden themselves, Freud and his followers offered "scientific" evidence that there were right and wrong ways of handling the responsibility.

But it was the work of a lesser-known psychologist, Englishman John Bowlby, which took the circumstance of mothers' exclusive, round-the-clock contact with their children and converted it into a moral and psychological imperative. Bowlby had done research in British orphanages following World War II, in which he found that many institutionalized babies lost all interest in play or even eating. Even partially deprived of maternal care, Bowlby concluded in a 1951 World Health Organization brief, children could develop "anxiety, excessive need for love, powerful feelings of revenge, and, arising from these last, guilt and depression."* Complete deprivation would have even more acute effects and might entirely cripple the child's ability to form relationships.

The babies Bowlby studied weren't simply deprived of "maternal" love, however. Though fed and kept clean, they weren't often held and were never even given the chance to form stable relationships with the nurses who cared for them. Somehow, the details of Bowlby's studies were overlooked, and instead of confirming the notion that babies need warm, continuous relationships of *some* kind, the work became "scientific evidence" that the *mother's* warm, continuous presence was essential to every baby's development.

A generation of American women stayed home to do Bowlby's bidding. By the late 1960s, however, an enormous backlash had taken shape and was sweeping the country in the form of the women's movement. Men's work was more fulfilling than raising babies, the feminists said (or seemed to say). Combined with the inflations and recessions of the 1970s, it was enough to chase women back into the job market in record numbers. And day-care became a fact of life.

That is, more or less, where we stand today. Whereas our ancestors led a life in which children and work were well integrated (if not more "fulfilling"), we are trapped between the contradictory legacies of Bowlby and feminism. Because of Bowlby, we'll always worry that something terrible could happen to our babies if we return to work. Because of feminism, we'll worry that if we choose the babies, something terrible could happen to us.

Making the Choice

A Twenty-nine-Year-Old Mother of Six-Week-Old Twins:

I've always wanted to be a mom. Of all the different jobs I've had, as a secretary and a receptionist and a salesperson,

---

* John Bowlby, *Child Care and the Growth of Love*, Penguin Books, 1953.

I've loved them all. But they weren't what I wanted to do with the rest of my life. This—motherhood—is what I've been aiming for.

A Twenty-nine-Year-Old Bank Executive, Mother of a Five-Month-Old:

I always just assumed that I was going back to work. When the time came to actually return after my maternity leave, I started to feel a little unsure. But I knew I was going to do it anyway, regardless of feeling unsure. Because I have a good job, something I've worked hard to get, and I didn't want to just give it up. If I were to just sit home with my child all week, like I do on weekends—well, I love it, but it's not stimulating at all. It doesn't test my limits and my education.

Not that I want to keep working full-time forever, necessarily. But I can always decide to quit later, whereas if I quit now and want to come back later, that would be hard to do.

In between the group of women born to mother and the group that fits (at least mentally) into their pre-pregnancy business suits six weeks after birth is a large gray swamp where the rest of us flounder. It's not that we don't have strong feelings on the subject; the problem is, our strong feelings contradict one another.

Usually, the decision about whether or not to stay with a job involves weighing your ideas about day-care against your family's financial need and/or your emotional and intellectual investment in your career. Here are some of the questions you may be asking yourself:

■ *"Is Day-Care a Good Idea?"* To what extent does an infant need an intense, continuous relationship with a parent in order to develop "normally"? How much intellectual stimulation does he need, and can he get it in a group situation? What kinds of values might he be absorbing during fifty or sixty hours a week in someone else's company?

These are all good questions. But if you expect definitive answers, you're out of luck. Researches are, of course, hacking away at them. But so far, their findings tend to contradict one another, and there hasn't been time yet for the sorts of studies that might shed light on the long-term effects of day-care.

Even if there were such studies available now, I would take them with barrels and barrels of salt. Your child isn't a statistic, and it won't make any difference how 78 percent of children react in a given situation if yours is in the other 22 percent.

Abstract thought in general is a bad basis for decision on this subject. Many women say they're paralyzed merely by the *idea* of day-care, which is so intimidating or downright terrifying that they can't bring themselves to actually start investigating alternatives.

The day-care decision should be based on gut feelings, which in turn should be based on personal investigation. Once you see the facilities available to you, meet the person or people who'd be caring for your baby, see how other children look in the setting you're considering, and talk to other parents about their experiences, you probably won't have too much trouble making up your mind. (For more on the pros and cons of specific arrangements, and suggestions on how to start your search, see chapter 11.)

■ *"How Much Money Do We Need?"*   Do you *need* to earn a salary? If you can't guarantee food on the table and a roof over your head otherwise, obviously you do.

But "need" is an elastic concept reflecting a whole set of ideas about what you want out of life beyond a full belly and dry hair. You may *need* a job order to live in a decent neighborhood where there aren't crack dealers on the street corners. You may also *need* to work to pay the mortgage on a house in a charming suburban historic neighborhood, if that's where you want to live. The chances are good that you will *need* to work merely in order to sustain the life-style you grew up with (while your mother was staying home to raise you).

These needs are all legitimate. But they aren't written in stone. If you're considering going back to work *only* because of financial need, you might want to sit down and rethink your *immediate* needs. Do you have to buy a home *now*? Can it wait until the kids are in school and you can go back to a job with a lighter conscience? Remember that staying home will decrease some of your expenses: You won't need expensive clothes, lunches out, transportation, fast-food dinners, and, of course, day-care.

You might also want to rethink your philosophical needs. Sometimes women who've prided themselves on contributing equally or substantially to the joint expenses feel that quitting would be tantamount to freeloading on their husbands.

Well, it would be sort of retro, but is it freeloading? If you think so, try staying home for a week and see how hard you think you're working. If your husband thinks so, let *him* try it for a week.

▪ *"Will I Be Happy as a Full-Time Mom?"*   This is a perfectly legitimate question. If you've been bored by your work, if you've bounced from job to job without feeling much commitment to anything, if you've begun to wonder what all those feminists were screaming about, having a baby is a wonderful excuse to bow out of the world of crass commerce for a while and devote yourself to something—and someone—you truly care about.

But that thinking works both ways. If you love what you do, if you're burning up with ambition, if being financially independent is essential to your self-esteem, those are needs you have to treat respectfully. No matter how much you love your baby, raising her all by yourself isn't going to help you get rich or famous or find a cure for cancer. Raising her all by yourself is going to make you often exhausted and perhaps bored and will certainly allow you plenty of time to dwell on your lost dreams. And you have to ask yourself whether your baby wouldn't be better off in warm, cheerful substitute care at least part of the time while you do what you need to do to be happy during the time you're with her.

Living with Your Choice

Whichever choice you make, be prepared for a period of adjustment that may take months. Quitting your job isn't going to provide instant relief, like playing hooky from algebra. And the job you return to won't be the exact same job you left—or at least your attitude toward it will probably change in ways that surprise you.

Here's what women in both camps have said about learning to live with their decisions:

Staying Home

■ *Lack of Accomplishment, Lack of Feedback.* No matter how badly you wanted to do it, staying home with a baby all day requires a major shift of mental gears. Up to now, you've functioned in a world of measurable, rewardable achievements. When you were in school, you took tests and wrote papers and got grades. If you were athletic, you practiced and trained and then you won or lost. When you got a job, you met quotas or got evaluated or perhaps merely got ranted at by a horrible boss; at any rate, you usually knew where you stood, and your paycheck was tangible evidence that you had accomplished something as time went by. All along, you've been trained to function in a world where glory would come unto you if you gave your best.

In the world of the full-time mommy, this kind of thinking will get you nowhere. Especially in the early months, when the baby is at its most demanding and least responsive, the arrangement usually requires you to pour oceans of energy, patience, and time in, and get very little in return. Not only can you *not* expect positive feedback, you are extremely likely to get negative feedback. The baby is going to cry inexplicably at least some of the time and possibly a great deal of the time, and suggestions from the well intentioned may sound like criticism to your praise-starved ears.

I had always thought of myself at work as the kind of person who could always deliver. But with the baby, I felt all I was doing was washing and changing diapers and no one was thanking me. And there were no answers to so many questions, like why was he crying? Every six weeks or so, I'd visit the pediatrician, and he'd say, "Oh, you're doing fine," and I'd leave there feeling really good. And then after a while, all the bad feelings would start coming back.

It makes me angry how hard it is to shrug aside all the conditioning we've had that equates worth with income. However much I try to tell myself that staying home and taking care of Max is a worthwhile thing to do, I don't quite believe it. My husband comes home and asks what I did all day and I say, "Nothing."

I was in grad school working on my master's before I had her. Now my challenges are: Can I make dinner and also get the housework done? Can I give the baby a bath before I have to go out? My husband doesn't expect an ideal housewife, with a hot dinner on the table when he comes home. I put the pressure on myself. I feel that since I'm home, I should be able to manage all the housework and the meals and the shopping and the errands. But I really can't, yet.

I love being a mom. I don't miss working. But defining my new self is hard. At work, you could always say: "I got this report written; I attended this meeting." I guess I could say, "I gave her this many bottles and changed this many diapers," but it's not quite the same thing.

In the beginning, I found myself making a list every day and leaving it on the table, hoping that my husband would see it and know that I had accomplished something during the day. Then he said, "Why are you so worried about getting the floor scrubbed? Your job is taking care of the baby."

Trying to scale down your expectations is a good way of dealing with the frustration of life with an infant. After all, while accomplishing almost nothing may not be normal for *you*, it is perfectly normal for a woman in your situation, as the other women in this book testify. Ultimately, these feelings will start to fade. For one thing, you'll begin to forget about the pace of your old life and find things to appreciate in the pace of your new one. And as the baby gets older and more independent, you'll begin to be able to accomplish more of what you want to do.

▪ *Feeling Isolated.*   It's ironic that feelings of isolation and loneliness are so universal among new mothers. But whether you live in an apartment building with a hundred other families or out in the country on your own hundred acres, having a baby immediately sets you apart from your old life and from many of the people you called friends.

I don't miss my job, but I miss the people I worked with. It's very difficult to keep up those contacts when you're leading a life at home, even though I'm still living in Manhattan and they all work here. My life is so different from theirs, and usually the time I could talk to them on the phone, when he's napping, is the time they're out to lunch, literally. At night I just don't have the energy to call up someone I haven't talked to in six months.

The only people who kept calling me were the ones who were also mothers and really understood what I was going through, and they were really the only ones I wanted to talk to. The others didn't have a clue. They couldn't understand being so tired that you could barely pick up a phone.

The first couple of weeks were really hard. We only have one car, so in order to get it I have to get up at 5:00 in the morning to drive my husband to work. He came home the other night and I was crying, and I told him, "I have got to have that car at least one day a week. Even if it's just to drive to the supermarket for a loaf of bread. I just need to get out and see people."

Now it's not so bad. One day a week I go to a new mother's group, and one day I take the car and do errands. But I had to make a conscious effort.

I'm going a little nuts out here in the country. I have a friend who just moved here and she's still in shock. She keeps asking, "Where's the park? Where's the playground?" I keep telling her, "Here, you use your backyard."

One way I've figured out to meet some other mothers is by baby-sitting for the garden club and the Republican Women's Club. It's two or three days a month, and it means she gets to see other babies and I've gotten a few phone numbers of mothers who might be willing to exchange some sitting time. Everyone out here has a problem getting sitters, especially if they have more than one kid.

The silver lining in the cloud of isolation is that of all the problems of new motherhood, it's probably the easiest one to do something about. Because the feeling *is* universal, you can count on the fact that there are a few women in your immediate neighborhood who are dying to get together and talk feeding, development, pediatricians, and husbands. (To find them, see the suggestions in chapter 4, pages 65–66).

▪ *Unaccustomed Dependence on Your Husband.*   One side effect of both the frustrating and isolating aspects of early motherhood is that suddenly, for a while, your husband may become your lifeline to everything: positive feedback, love, financial support, plain social contact. This can be scary for women who've worked hard to develop an independent identity if they jump to the conclusion that the dependence will be permanent.

By 4:30 P.M., if I haven't seen anyone all day, I usually can't wait for my husband to get home. But his job is really demanding. On a good day, he'll be home at 6:30, but he never knows what his hours will be, and some days he calls at 6:00 and says,

"Looks like I won't get home till nine." And on days when I'm really going stir-crazy, I'll bundle her up and get in the car and go to my mom's for dinner.

I find myself falling into all these 1950s sitcom patterns with my husband. Especially in the first few weeks, I was nagging a lot more. I think it's because I couldn't get out to do anything. He'd do an errand and come home with the wrong thing, and I'd fly off the handle, because I couldn't go get it myself. And suddenly, I notice that I'm very territorial about domestic turf. Like, the kitchen is *my* domain, which is odd, because we've always shared the cooking. We've always shared everything, but suddenly I'm worried about what's for dinner and he's really worried about his paycheck.

The kind of desperate dependence you feel about needing to see your husband walk in the door at exactly the second you expect him is usually fairly short-lived. For most women, it seems to disappear between six weeks and three months, around the time the baby stops doing long stretches of unexplained crying and allows you substantial chunks of sleep at night. This is also the point at which you're more likely to be getting out on your own and meeting other new mothers.

But there are other feelings of dependence which are much more deep-rooted. Financial dependence, for example, can be very uncomfortable for women who are used to supporting themselves. It may be that after a few months, you stop thinking about it. Or you may realize that it's extremely important to you to go back to earning money. If you've always had separate bank accounts and yours is now fast deflating, the solution may be to renegotiate the finances, giving you equal control over his income, on the theory that both his wage earning and your child rearing are joint ventures.

This brings up the issue one new mother called the "1950s sitcom pattern" of marriage, in which he brings home the bacon and you fry it, as you swore in high school you never would.

Embedded in all of us is the image of "proper" parenting we grew up with, whether we consciously approved of it or not. If that included a daddy who worked and a mommy who stayed home, then that's probably an arrangement your heart sympathizes with, even if your head is skeptical.

It's an undeniable fact that this life-style requires you to be financially dependent on your husband. If your relationship is good and you can trust he'll stick around long-term and you don't have to beg for your allowance and you both respect what you're trying to give the baby by staying at home, it won't feel much like dependence after a while. But if it does, you need to rethink staying home.

▪ *Loss of Personal Freedom.* You don't have to have been one of those people who went dancing every night or enjoyed backpacking in Tibet to feel an acute loss of spontaneity after the birth of a child. You need only to be one of those people who occasionally finds it necessary to go to the supermarket and buy milk and eggs, a process that can become complex and terrifying in the first weeks of motherhood.

Generally, hankering after your lost life-style is most severe in those early weeks. In part, this is simply because you still clearly remember your old life and haven't come to take the inconveniences of working around a baby's needs in stride, as you probably will. But it's also true that going anywhere with a newborn is a logistical feat involving intricate planning of feeding schedules and equipment.

I had traveled all the time in my job, and my husband and I loved to go away together for weekends. The first time we traveled with him, he was nine days old and we were going to our house in the country. I felt very brave for going, but we had about twelve fights on our way out of the house over what we should take with us. We looked like we were going to Europe for a few months. We looked like we could use a Mack truck. And here was this one tiny little baby at the bottom of it all. We were crazed, but he slept the entire way.

The next time, we only took half as much stuff. But we've also started to ask ourselves when the impulse to travel hits, "Do we really want to get in the *car?*"

There's some good news and some bad news on this subject. In some ways, it becomes easier to get the baby out as she grows older (although it's always harder in winter than summer because of all the extra layers). Once she's on solid foods, you don't have to worry so much about the constant possibility of having to make a breast-feeding pit stop; you also don't have to worry so much about extra clean clothes for diaper-overflow situations, since the stools harden considerably; and once she's off formula you can pretty much count on being able to get her something to eat or drink anywhere you go. Also, the older she gets, the more willing you'll probably feel to leave her with sitters at least occasionally.

On the other hand, the nice thing about infants is that they sleep so much and so indiscriminately. Once she's awake most of the day—especially once she's mobile—it won't be so easy to take her into a store for more than ten minutes at a time. Once she stops sleeping through all car trips, you'll have to do some heavy-duty entertaining to keep her happy. And once she's walking, she won't sit still—or, better yet, sleep—through dinners out.

I came home from the hospital on a Sunday night, and Tuesday we went to a restaurant. We took her with us. I called ahead, made reservations for early, 5:30. I told them I wanted a no-smoking table in a corner, far removed from the other tables. I said, "I'm bringing a beautiful, well-behaved infant and I'm spending at least a hundred bucks and I want it to be nice." I spent $103, and it was beautiful.

■ *Feeling Dowdy.* For some women, throwing away panty hose and high-heeled shoes is one of the major rewards of quitting work. The kinds of clothes you can wear around a baby—the kinds of clothes that can get spit up on and drooled on with no cata-strophic consequences—tend to be the most comfortable clothes

on earth, so if freedom of movement is what you're after, welcome
to the wonderful world of sweat suits.

But for most women, the joy of liberation from dressing for
success is mixed with a slightly sick sense of having swung too far
off in the opposite direction.

I just don't seem to have the energy to worry about those
last five pounds I should lose. I used to be the kind of person
who worried when my nails weren't perfect. Now, I couldn't
care less. I wear the same clothes over and over and over—the
few that fit and that I don't mind having her spit up on. I have
a whole closet full of things that are too tight or too dressy, but
I'm not shopping for anything new. I'm letting the closet remind me that I'll have to do something about my weight.

When I worked, I'd put on nice clothes, makeup, do my
hair. Now, I take a shower every day, but there isn't time to
spend on getting myself spruced up.

I definitely don't feel as sexy as I used to. And it's partly the
extra weight. Right now I'm still in my fat clothes. You know
the ones you have from when you've been really good on your
diet and you can go out and buy a pair of jeans that fit you like
a glove? I'm not in those. I'm in the ones you have from when
you blimped out for a while.

Being home all day makes it somewhat harder to fix yourself up
again after birth. You don't *have* to fit back into your tight clothes
right away. You're functioning in extremely close proximity to the
refrigerator, and while you seem to be exhausted most of the time,
it's not from the sort of aerobic exertion that sculpts model-shaped
bodies. If you're feeling bored and isolated, the depression may
drive you to seek comfort in snacking as you console yourself with
the thought that your nursing will burn up "lots" of extra calories.

The important thing to remember is that post-childbirth frump-
iness is almost universal (Princesses Di and Caroline excepted, but
look at all the professional help they have), and that it is also

temporary. That doesn't mean that *eventually* you won't have to work at making it go away. But eventually you'll have more energy and self-discipline than you have now. Eventually, the baby won't be spitting up on you. Eventually, you'll figure out some way of getting exercise—daily walks with or without the baby, jogs while a neighbor watches him, an aerobics class at a health facility with a baby-sitting service, a videotape you can work out with when you get up.

It's not a bad idea to take a few morale-boosting steps now. These might include a special treat, like a haircut, perm, facial, manicure, or massage. If it cheers you to see yourself made up, make the time for a quickie session. And get yourself one or two comfortable, attractive, stretchy, washable outfits even if you intend to lose lots more weight—just so you don't go around feeling so depressed in the meantime that you end up pigging out more.

Once the rest of your life falls back into place, the willpower to put your appearance back together will well up inside you. The fact that this may not happen for months—for even a year or more—doesn't mean it won't happen. And you shouldn't be hard on yourself in the meantime, when you need the energy for more important things.

■ *Second-Guessing Your Decision.* One of the hardest things about being home full-time is that while it seems you don't have any time to get anything done, you do seem to have plenty of time to worry about what everyone else is doing.

> For years, I was a beat cop, and everyone in the department expected me to come right back to work. But that would be very hard for me. It was stressful and time-consuming. It would be hard to do it and also keep up my house. There are women on the force who do it, but they all have housekeepers. I think if you're going to pay someone to baby-sit, and pay someone to clean your house, what kind of parent are you? You're getting it all done for you, and you're missing out on it all.
>
> But it's still a hard decision. When you watch those TV

shows, there are so many women "having it all." I saw one the other night with a woman—a single mother—who was operating a day-care in her home and going to law school at night. And I thought, "How is she supposed to be doing this? How is she doing her homework from law school? Is she doing it while the day-care kids are there?" I mean, they show her really participating with the kids, so how could she?

It makes me feel dumb. How come I can't do that if so many women can? I seem to see it everywhere; I read about it all the time. But I feel that if I can get one single thing done during the day, it's been a really good day. This morning, it took me two hours to do the breakfast dishes.

The image of the Supermother haunts all mothers—those with full-time jobs as well as those who stay home. The main difference is that women who work full-time have *help*. It's true that they may not feel they get everything done as well as they should, and it's also true they're trying to do more than the woman who stays home. But any women who feels inadequate comparing herself to a professional mother should remember this: At home in that professional mother's kitchen, or in a day-care home or center, is another woman who can't get out to do her grocery shopping or get her own house cleaned or sit down and read a magazine because *she's* so busy looking after the professional woman's baby.

The difference, in other words, isn't between what two "kinds" of women are capable of achieving. The difference is what a specified amount of baby-sitting time will allow you to achieve.

Also keep in mind that nothing you see on TV or read in magazines on this subject is really true. Popular stories, fiction or nonfiction, almost inevitably simplify issues in the interest of making a stronger point. Editors like success stories, and producers like happy endings. Neither is terribly interested in the real lives of people who muddle through as best they can.

Finally, remember the hackneyed advice of Polonius to his son in *Hamlet:* "To thine own self be true." If you've decided that you care more about raising your child than about making the right career moves, don't be one of those people who bemoans society's lack of respect for stay-at-home mothers. The only way to change this lack of respect is for mothers to respect themselves.

You don't have to be obnoxious about it. You don't have to chew people's ears off at cocktail parties with the details of starting solid foods or proselytize job-holding mothers to stay home. But there's no reason ex-colleagues you run into on the street who ask, "What are you doing these days?" have to be mumbled at and apologized to.

When I first decided to stay home, I really felt I was bucking a trend. But now I think more people are starting to feel the way I do. At least, I've never felt I had to apologize for what I'm doing.

At my Lamaze class reunion, which was actually three classes together, I would say about 75 percent of the women in the room felt very frustrated about what they were doing. The ones who'd gone back to the office had a very hard time making it through every day. The ones who'd decided to stay home felt the need to apologize to everyone who asked them what they were up to these days. That disturbed me, and I told them so.

But I also think it's important to say I don't regard myself as a housewife. And if I'm not a housewife, what am I? When I run into people who ask what I've been up to, my answer usually is: "I'm being a mother, and this is the hardest work I've ever done in my life."

Old Wives' Tales

"I missed my baby."

Kathleen returned to a high-powered job after a two-month maternity leave, only to decide a few months later that staying with her baby was more important.

The Joys of the Stay-at-Home Mother

▪ You can take life at the baby's pace, instead of forcing the baby to conform to your pace.

▪ You're around during the baby's "quality time," whenever it may happen to be.

▪ You can control the kinds of values and stimulation the baby is exposed to.

▪ You have time to talk to other mothers.

▪ You don't have to dress up, commute, punch a clock, or worry about what your boss thinks.

▪ You may have more time and energy to put into creating a warm, inviting home: to cook, bake, entertain.

▪ You may clarify your priorities for money, work, family, and time.

I had been with the company for twelve years. My job involved lots of travel and late nights in the city. When I was pregnant, I had managed to get other people to do a lot of that for me, but when I came back after the baby, I realized I was going to have to go back to doing my share. That wasn't the main reason I quit, but it was a factor. The main reason was that I missed my baby.

We live in the suburbs, so with my commute into the city, my working day was twelve hours long. I left the house before she was awake, and I'd come home and she might already be ready for bed. I never fed her a meal. I'd give her her bedtime bottle, and that was it. I could go a whole week without changing a diaper.

When I had thought about it abstractly, before I had her, it was very clear that I'd have the baby, get live-in help, and go back to work. From talking to other people who commute, it seemed that live-in help was the only alternative. When you have to be on that early train, you can't be standing at the front door waiting for a sitter with car trouble. The only way you can be sure of a person being there is when they've slept over the night before. So that's what I did, and the girl I hired was great with the baby.

But having someone live in your house isn't so easy. I had a girl in her twenties, and she had her own problems and her own friends. I felt it was an intrusion, and we have a fairly large home. She had her own living quarters in the basement. She used my car, and her friends would call her on the phone, and, you know, it's just another person you have to talk to when you don't feel like it. It's not like she really hung around with us. She'd go into her own rooms in the evening, and she'd go away with her friends on weekends. And it was really nice to be able to decide on the spur of the moment that we felt like going out to a movie, without needing to call up ten people to ask if they could baby-sit. So it was certainly convenient. But I never really got used to having this extra person in the house.

I'll never forget my first day of going back to work. I just sat on the train and cried. When I left the house in the morning, I couldn't even go into the baby's room to say good-bye. I remember every day being on the train and feeling like I couldn't wait to get home. I couldn't get into the house fast enough.

I didn't expect leaving her to be that tough. I also found that it was very hard for me to feel motivated in my job. I would think, "This is so ridiculous. What's important is my baby." This was the type of job that really involved a lot of energy, and if you didn't care about it, it was much tougher to do than if you did care.

I'm very fortunate in that I never had to worry about how we'd pay the bills if I quit. But it was still a hard decision. The prevailing feeling in my company was that you had a baby and then you simply came back a few months later. At least, the high-level women came back. The people who stayed home with their babies were the secretaries.

And I really felt comfortable in that job; being a mother was a job I knew nothing about. Even though we'd been living in this town for five years, I didn't know anyone here. When you leave the house at 6:45 A.M. and don't come back for twelve hours, you don't meet people around home. All my friends were in the city. They all worked. Only now, a year later, do I really feel that I'm starting to know people out here.

It was very hard to be home in the beginning. Every morning, I'd go through this thing of, "Should I put makeup on or shouldn't I?" Sometimes I'd just stand there, trying to decide what to wear, and then I'd think, "Who cares? Who's going to see you, anyway?"

In my former life, I was very active, and I had this tremendous sense of accomplishment. Now, I'm still busy all the time, but I feel like I get nothing done. There are days when if I get to the grocery store and do something else, too, I feel, "Wow, I've gotten *so* much done." And sometimes three days will go by before I can even manage to get to the bank. It was tremendously frustrating to me that I couldn't get such simple things done.

And it's not like I feel like I'm good at doing new things. Am I *good* at changing diapers? Am I *good* at taking her to the swings? Well, I don't think I'm *bad* at it, but I don't think I'm good at it either. And a lot of days I feel guilty that I didn't play with Play-Doh, that I didn't create a thing for her to do. Or I'll feel guilty that she hasn't had a green vegetable in five days. Can she live on grilled cheese sandwiches for the rest of her life? And I dwell on these things because I'm a full-time mom.

It's funny how you start doing all those things you swore you'd never do. Like, the TV is on all the time in my house. She's totally fascinated with it, and I can get things done while she's watching it. And I thought I'd never be the kind of person who'd let my kid run loose in a store, but I do. Otherwise, I can't look at anything. And I swore I'd never be the kind of person who rips open boxes of crackers in the supermarket, and I do that now the minute I walk into the store, because otherwise I can't get her through the shopping.

I have no regrets at all about having quit. I've had the career. I have no desire to go back to that kind of life.

But I don't particularly like finding myself in the "Homemaker/Housewife" category, either. I don't like the terminology. My husband recently had a school reunion, and they sent a program with information on all the people in his class. I guess he must have filled out a form, because there under my occupa-tion was "housewife." I told him that next time he has to put down a title for me, he should put down "retired executive" or something.

I actually love being home, though. I love not needing to answer to a boss. I love being with my child, even though some days we drive each other crazy, and we get incredibly excited just to see other people. It's silly to say I'm "not working," because I feel like I'm working harder than I ever have in my life.

"I'll feel guilty no matter what I do."

Dora had a well-paid job wrapping meat in the butcher department of a major supermarket. She assumed she'd have to return for financial reasons and that she wouldn't really mind doing it. Once she had the baby, she decided she'd rather budget and pinch pennies—but she can't quite shake the feel-ing she *should* be able to do it all.

The decision not to return from maternity leave was really traumatic for me. The part that bothered me the most is that nobody really seemed to understand what I was going through. My coworkers all just expected me to come back to work. Nobody considered that I might want to stay home. When I brought up the possibility, everyone seemed really surprised, and that made me feel worse, like there was something wrong with me for want-ing to do it.

But after the baby was here and I saw how helpless he really was and how important I was for him, I started leaning toward not going back. The whole economic climate now encourages the idea that it's perfectly okay to put your kids in day-care. But we don't know what's going to happen to this whole generation. People are eager to do it without waiting to see what the consequences might be. I felt the sitter would have to be someone very close to me in order for me to trust her. I couldn't get over that awful barrier of calling up strangers to interview them. I just couldn't face it.

So I started thinking about how I could swing it financially. And I was really examining our life-style. I sat down and made a list of pluses and minuses, and I realized that staying home really was more important than the money. I sat up nights, losing sleep, worrying about it. In the end, I'd say it came more from the heart than from the head. I decided to quit.

At first I loved being home. Then I went through this stage of thinking I'd made a huge mistake. Because I didn't really know people, and I felt really alone. It's not as though I'd had close friends at work; I was the only woman in most of the departments I worked in. But at least I saw other adults. Now I'm having to learn to make friends with women. So I'm trying to get out and join some of those groups, like La Leche League and one of those mother-baby exercise classes. The isolation is awful, especially in the winter.

Financially, it's working out okay. I guess when I worked I'd just gotten used to having too much money and spending it. When you start making out budgets and thinking about where you're spending money, you can do it. Now, we've decided we can afford to buy a house, but we won't spend money other ways. We won't go out as much as we used to—but we wouldn't with the baby anyway. He won't go out to bars with his buddies; he'll have them over. I was never that extravagant before. But I certainly wouldn't have ever clipped coupons before. I thought it was really dorky. Now I definitely do that. I mean, I'm not one of those people that spends a lot of time on it, but I use the ones that are for brands I like.

I've realized that I'll feel guilty no matter what I do. I thought that if I didn't go back to work, I'd be guilty of not making extra money to spend on the baby. But if I did go back to work, I'd feel guilty about not being with the baby. And now, if I don't get everything done in a day that I want to, I feel guilty. The Super-woman thing is a big problem for me. Maybe it's just in my own mind, but I keep thinking other people are looking at me and wondering, "How come she doesn't have herself together?"

I'm prepared to go back to work part-time if things don't work out. Because I don't want to just live for the house, either. But I'm really trying to change my priorities. I'm trying to value people instead of things. I didn't realize how much I used to live just to buy material goods.

Working a Full-Time or Demanding Part-Time Job Outside The Home

- *Lack of Time.*

I didn't see a full-time working schedule as a problem before I had the baby. I thought, "Oh, the baby will just fit into my life and everything will work out." But when I went back to my job, I felt I had no time for myself, or for her. I found myself waking up at 5:00 in the morning, and then at 4:30, to get things done. And then I would stay up late so I could spend time with my husband. He and I would have these big discussions about how the housework needed to be divided up fairly. If he didn't do something on his list, it would make me hysterical. Finally, I decided to cut back to part-time work, and only once I did that was I able to see that I'd been trying to do too much.

There's not much flexibility in the schedule of the average working mother. Your employer sets your hours, your husband's sets his, the sitter or day-care center tells you when you have to come get your baby, and then you have all those errands that can only be done during store hours. Even your vacation time may get eaten away by obligations: sick days home with the baby, or trips to show the baby off to grandparents.

You may begin to look longingly at women who stay home all day with their babies, who presumably bake cookies, cook gourmet meals, spend unlimited "quality time" with their infants, and use nap times to keep up with all the latest fiction.

Don't fall into this trap. While it's true that exhaustion and frustration might be signs that you really would prefer being home, be forewarned that being home won't give you "more time" to get things done. It might, in fact, give you less time, because unless you've got regular access to affordable sitting, you'll be at the baby's mercy constantly, and that means you fulfill the baby's needs constantly, not your own. What being home might do, if your priorities have shifted, is give you the sense that your time is being spent on the thing that matters most to you.

Possible compromise solutions include cutting back to part-time work if you can, or quitting to start your own business out of your home. Also, you might begin to prune your errand time by taking advantage of mail-order catalogs and delivery services. If battles over major household chores are a regular feature of your marital relations, look into hiring cleaning people.

▪ *Guilt and Resentment.* Just as women who stay home full-time often struggle with a vague sense that they *ought* to be able to earn money *and* fulfill all the domestic responsibilities, women who don't want to be working full-time are often plagued by the sense that they *have* to. In this case, you find yourself feeling restlessly angry at whoever or whatever forced you into the situation, which may include your husband's inadequate earning power, the economy, your company's refusal to let you work part-time, or your brainwashing by misguided feminists.

> I saved enough money so I could take off a year. Going back is very hard for me. I've felt a lot of anger and resentment toward my husband about it, even though I realize that's stupid and illogical. But we can't afford for me to stay home.

And when I do go back, I'm going to have to scale down my ambitions because I won't have the time required for a management position. That makes me mad, because I feel I have a lot to offer, and if I were a man, I wouldn't have to make this choice.

Today there are so many *issues* involved with having children. Like, in the fifties, no one thought about going back to work. They just stayed home because that's what you did. And now, in the suburbs, people are starting to stay home again. It makes me feel like, "Oh-oh, the rules have changed again." And I feel left out, and doubly sad that I have to go back.

The other obvious target for the resentment of women who don't want to be working is the baby's caretaker. And it isn't simply the idea of the baby's attachment to a stranger that can be threatening; an obvious preference for anyone other than *us* is hard for most mothers to accept.

This seems really sick, but I'm very jealous of my husband's relationship with Zachary. In most normal Middle American families, you see the mommy and the baby going off to the supermarket together, and at night Daddy comes home and pats the baby on the head and reads the newspaper and goes to sleep.

In our family, it's just the opposite. I come home at night, and they've learned a new song or game, and they have to teach me.

Somehow, I get the feeling I never really had a chance to bond with Zachary. Certainly, I think he loves me and I love him. But sometimes I don't really feel like I'm his mother. George can make this kid laugh by doing *anything*. But because of the small amount of time I have with him, I try to force the issue: I instantly want him to laugh or say "Mama." They have all the time in the world, and that makes me jealous.

There are a few possibilities for dealing with the guilt, resentment, and jealousy of having to work when you don't want to.

First, be aware that every mother seems to have some of these feelings no matter what her life-style. Every working mother sometimes misses her baby while she's away and fantasizes about spending more time together—just as every stay-at-home mother at least occasionally would rather be anywhere on earth other than her own kitchen.

Second, if you're struggling with a lot of these feelings in anticipation of going back to work, you should know that contemplating separation and day-care are often far worse than actually experiencing them. Don't assume the situation is going to be unbearable until you've actually begun living with it, and then give it a little time to see if you can all sink comfortably in.

If it does feel unbearable, then it's time to reexamine your ideas about why you "have" to work and see whether you can't actually scale down your life-style to fit one salary—or whether you can't scale down your working time.

- *Trouble Dealing with the Sitter/Day-Care.* There's a difference between the way you deal with someone hired to care for your child and the way you might deal with someone hired, say, to fix your car.

A sitter is sort of somewhere in between a family member and an employee. I don't quite know how to deal with my sitter sometimes. When I come home, I'm tired, and if she's forgotten to empty the diaper pail or she's messed up the kitchen without cleaning up, I'll get mad, but I won't say anything. Part of me wants to scream at her, but she's very defensive. But then, when my husband gets home, I'll bitch at him and take it out on him.

I know I'm not as patient with her as I'd be with someone at the office. But I also wouldn't have any qualms about telling someone in the office, "Hey, you really screwed up on this; don't do it again." And they wouldn't take it personally. But

my friends and I are slaves to our baby-sitters. If we bring
something up, they threaten to quit. And what are we going to
do if she up and quits tomorrow with no notice? I can't force
her to give me two weeks' notice.

There are those who might argue that brusquely telling a subordinate, "You really screwed up on this; don't do it again," dis-
plays less-than-optimal management skill, even in an office
environment. The only real difference between an office employee
and a sitter is that the office environment reinforces the idea that
an employee has to put up with a boss's treatment, even if it's
rude, irrational, and disrespectful.

But it's not simply because sitters are so hard to come by
that you need to treat yours with respect. In the first place, you
shouldn't ever hire someone you don't respect to have sole responsibility for your baby. And if you don't have the self-
discipline to treat the sitter respectfully even when you're mad
or upset, is it fair to expect the sitter to have the self-discipline
to treat your child respectfully, even when the sitter's in a bad
mood?

On the other hand, any health or safety problems need to
be dealt with immediately and firmly. This means that, if on
picking the baby up one day you find the front door unlocked or
see a package of mothballs lying out on the coffee table, you don't
worry about being polite. You say something, immediately, and if
the sitter doesn't take it seriously, you start looking for another
sitter.

It also means standing up for your child at all times. If, for
instance, the day-care center suddenly starts talking about "be-
havioral problems," don't just accept the labels; she could be
responding to something about the care she's receiving. Schedule
a conference; find out how much and when they're letting her
nap, and how often she's getting someone's individual attention.

In other words, it's important to swallow your irrational emotional reaction (your jealousy, and whatever frustration you've

built up during the day at work) at all costs. And when you need to deal with those health, safety, and happiness issues, raise them gently.

■ *Changed Attitudes toward Work.* Look around you at the men in positions of power. Do they have children? Probably. Do they have wives? Probably. Do the wives work? Probably not—or, at least, they didn't when the children were young.

It's an unfortunate fact that "excellence," as it is commonly conceived of in modern American business, is presumed to include very long working hours and a slavish commitment to the company. Lots of women are willing to compete with male colleagues on those terms—until they have babies. Then, one of two things usually happens: The woman decides she can't match the commitment of male colleagues who have wives caring for them and their children; or the company decides the woman can't match the commitment of male colleagues who have wives caring for them and their children. Even in situations where the latter decision is illegal, it happens all the time.

Either way, having a baby is likely to test the limits of your ambition.

Originally, before I went on maternity leave, I had a management job. I could have kept it if I had decided to come back full-time, but I only wanted to come back part-time, so I gave it up, even though the position meant a lot to me.

Two weeks ago, they offered it to me again, and this time they said I could do it part-time. So I had to go through the whole agony of deciding again. Ultimately, I decided that it would just be another source of anxiety and conflict, because it really *is* a full-time job. I don't think I could have done it well in the time I had to do it, and I'm sure I would have ended up working a lot more than I was being paid for because I would have felt it just had to get done. But for a while there, my ego was screaming, "It's tremendous! I can 'have it all'! I can have my old job back *and* have my baby!"

It's hard, because meanwhile I see people getting promoted all around me, and I can't help thinking those are jobs I would have had a shot at. On the other hand, I come home, and the baby goes crazy when he sees me, and then I feel like it's worth it.

I've been with this company for fifteen years. I started as a secretary and worked my way up. At this point, to let me go, they'd have to have a pretty damn good reason and a vice president's signature. But still, when I knew the baby was coming, I got it in writing that my job was still going to be there when I got back from maternity leave.

But in the fifth week of my six-week leave, my boss called and told me to report to a different office when I returned. I told him I'd go but I thought it stunk and I wanted that written down somewhere. Then, I had to miss a lot of work in the first two or three months because I had to take the baby to the hospital for physical therapy sessions. Plus I couldn't work late because I had to be at the sitter's to pick her up by 5:00. So I wasn't putting in anywhere near the hours I had been, and I don't think they liked that.

So then they decided to send me back to my old office, only instead of assigning me to the product I'd been working on, they assigned me to one they were phasing out. Basically, I felt they were demoting me. So I said, "And what's going to happen to me after that?"

Later that day, I got a call from my old boss, the one I chewed out over the phone, and he said he was going to be involved in a new-product launch, and after I wrapped up this dying product, I could come work for him again. So I asked, "Is there going to be a lot of overtime?" And he said, "I expect so."

I went home and thought about it. And I realized I don't want to work Saturdays, and I don't want to work nights. It's not that I respect my work less, but my priorities are just different now. So I said, "No."

Later, one woman took me aside and said, "They're shoving you aside. Don't let them do that. They're doing that to all the women." And I said, "Look, I can't do four to six hours of overtime a day. At this point in my life, I'm not trying to climb up any ladder. Right now, this is the best place for me."

■ *Feeling Fat.* One side effect of returning to a job is being forced to confront your working wardrobe with your postpartum breasts, hips, and thighs. You may find this depressing, especially since the last thing you have time for right now is aerobics.

I gained thirty-five pounds and I've only lost twenty. I have a sedentary job. I sit at a desk all day, and I drive back and forth, and when I get home, I sit on the couch and watch TV. My mother kept saying, "Oh, the weight will fall right off," but she lied. It's sitting right there on my hips. I have this big black skirt with an elastic waist, and my husband just noticed that I wear it three times a week. But I refuse to buy a whole new size-12 wardrobe, because then I'll get used to fitting into it.

You don't need to buy a whole new larger-size wardrobe. But it's not a bad idea to buy two or three elastic-waist skirts in versatile colors, just to take the pressure off yourself. It takes months—sometimes a year or more—before your life falls into place after having a baby. Once it has, losing the weight will probably be easier. But until then, you've got enough pressure on you without needing to be gorgeous, too.

Old Wives' Tales

"I have to punch a time clock to make my money."

Like many working women, Kim assumed when she was pregnant that her baby would fit neatly into the pattern of a life she was very comfortable with. Her husband, George, who disapproved of child care for infants, and who could be flexible about his own working schedule, agreed to do the daytime child care. But the baby's arrival threw all these rational decisions into a different perspective, and nine months into motherhood, Kim is ambivalent about both her working and mothering roles.

I don't think anyone really knows what's going to happen to their lives after the baby gets here, but I think I was possibly a little more naive than most. I'd just turned thirty, and I thought it was about time for motherhood. I expected nirvana, and I didn't think about anything negative.

My husband and I decided when I was pregnant that I would return to work full time after a six-week maternity leave. I'd been working on my career for the past few years and really didn't want to put it on hold. But the most important reason for returning was financial. George had just started his own business and he needs to reinvest all his profits to keep it going. And I've always been responsible for paying my share of the bills. Honestly, I'd say we didn't think about it that much. It was a given.

When I thought about how it would be, though, I only thought about the practical aspects. I commute an hour each way, and I worried about how I'd manage that every day. But I didn't think, "I'm the mommy, and the mommy is leaving her baby behind." In other words, I didn't think emotionally.

By the end of the maternity leave, I was really looking forward to getting out of the house and seeing other grown-ups and traveling again. But the morning I went back, I went into Zack's room and cried hysterically. I was like a little kid on the first day of school. I wanted to go, but I didn't want to go. I felt guilty, and I only wanted to go on my terms. But that's not the way employment works. When my boss signs my paycheck, he tells me when he wants me at work. They threw a big party for me at the office that day, with a cake and everything, and that really cheered me up. But I must have called home at least fifty times.

My job requires me to travel out of town for a whole week out of every month. And when I come back from my trips now, my family doesn't always seem happy to see me. George knows it's just part of the job, but he has to be with Zack twenty-four hours a day for that week and can't get any time to himself. The first couple of times, Zack would scream when he saw me and not let me hold him. Now he just gets very cranky, but he always makes me pay. And I'm starting to think it may not be worth it.

I think our division of domestic responsibilities is very fair. Normally, as soon as I walk in the door at night, George hands me the baby and says, "He needs a diaper; I'm off duty." I always fix Zack's dinner and read to him and put him to bed. And on weekends I have him 98 percent of the time because that's when George does a lot of his business.

And I think George is actually the better parent. He's never angry, and he's always very calm about everything. Once I was absolutely convinced that Zack was burning up with a 200-degree fever, and I was running around screaming, "Omigod, what do we do? Call the doctor!" And George very calmly went and got the thermometer, and Zack's temperature was normal, and two hours later he was laughing and playing as usual.

But I worry a lot about this idea of Supermom. I think it's the biggest piece of bull I've ever heard in my life. You cannot be glamorous and gorgeous and be an attorney and work twelve hours a day and come home and be a wonderful wife and wonderful mother and wonderful lover and only sleep two hours a night and still get up and get through your Jane Fonda workout. I've never met a person who was actually like that. You're going to forget to do something at work because something at home went wrong, or you're not going to lose your weight fast enough. I just don't think you can do it all. But there is that kind of pressure on young parents these days.

Still, I expect myself to be this superhuman person.

If I had my druthers, I wouldn't have gone back to work. I wouldn't have stayed home forever, either, because I think that could drive me nutty, too. My ideal situation would have been a year off.

But this is the deal I made with my husband. And he could afford to do it because he's flexible enough to make a living and still be with the baby 99 percent of the time. I can't do that. I have to punch a time clock to make my money.

"I couldn't wait to get back to work."

Becky also never thought very seriously about doing anything other than returning to her job after a brief maternity leave. And for her, six months into motherhood, the decision is extremely comfortable.

I was always going to go back to work. I like my job, and I don't see how we could make it financially otherwise. And I just couldn't imagine staying home. I function very well in a routine, and I was afraid that if I stayed home I'd just lapse into nonfunctioning.

I took an eight-week maternity leave, and I couldn't wait to get back to work. Exactly what I feared happened. Nine o'clock was *Leave It to Beaver;* 9:30 was *Lucy;* 10:00 was *Bewitched.* There were days I didn't even get dressed. I'd go out, feel like I had no purpose going out, and then just think, "I might as well go home."

Being home just wasn't like what I expected. I remember thinking I was going to get all this stuff done around the house, but it never happened. When I got home from the hospital, I had seven pounds to lose, and I thought, "Boy, this is going to be a breeze." But in the course of nursing, I gained another six. I was starving. I didn't eat between meals but I ate huge meals and drank lots of juice. And my chest was just gargantuan, like two watermelons. I never felt presentable. That's one of the reasons I quit nursing after a couple of weeks.

Having a baby hasn't changed my attitude toward work at all. I have the perfect job for having a baby. I work nine to five, and that's it. I've been doing it for twelve years. The only thing that's different now is that I sometimes fantasize staying home, say five to ten years in the future. I could see doing that when all the kids are in school, and I could have some free time. But for now, weekends are enough. I guess that sounds sort of mean, but I just don't know if I could do it every day. On the weekends, I don't always wash my face or brush my teeth. I don't always take the same care of myself that I do during the week, when I know someone is looking after him who gets paid to do it. You know, on the weekends sometimes, when my husband is taking care of the baby, I feel like I should rush to get back, so I don't overburden him.

I have a very reliable sitter who comes in every day from 8:00 A.M. to 6 P.M. She stays over if we want to go out at night, and has even stayed in the apartment with him while we went away for a weekend. I pay her about half my take-home salary.

I think every mother who has someone come in to care for the child worries that maybe the baby is going to like the sitter better or is going to think the sitter is his mother. Because she does spend more time with him than I do. But so far, although he clearly likes her, he doesn't seem to prefer her.

I don't know what I would do all day if I stayed home. I don't have that many friends who don't work full-time, so I don't know what adults I would ever see. And I like my job. It's fun, creative, stimulating. Not all the time, of course; all jobs are a pain in the neck sometimes. And I like getting paid.

Also, my husband is sort of chauvinistic. Every once in a while, he drops a hint about how he can't wait to be in charge. As though now I'm more an equal partner because I'm earning money. But every once in a while he'll say wouldn't it be nice if I were home all day? And I know that if I were, he'd constantly be saying, "Well, why didn't you do X or Y?"

I can't stand the idea of having to ask him for money. We have separate checking accounts, and we've always been pretty relaxed about who pays for what. But I'm a little afraid of what would happen if I stayed home. It's not that he's an ogre or anything, but independence is a big issue for me.

I just don't have any guilt about working. And I'll tell you what I think of that "quality time" issue. I was with my mother the other day, and I'd mentioned that I felt tired all the time, and at the end of the day she said, "I see why you're so tired. You are playing with that baby *all* the time. When he's happy, leave him alone. I know you're doing it because you don't see him during the week, so you feel you owe it to him. But if you were home all day long, you'd realize that you leave them alone a lot of the time. When you're at home doing the laundry, cleaning, you're not playing with the baby twenty-four hours a day. You're working a lot of the time." That made me feel a lot better, because I had felt that I had to be constantly entertaining him.

The funny thing is, it was so hard taking care of him in the beginning, but he's at a completely different stage now, and some times I think if he'd been this much fun when he was first born, I would never have gone back to work.

In terms of guilt, the only thing I can think of is that my mother was a great mother in every sense of the word. We had different colored cupcakes on every holiday, and gingerbread houses and Santa's workshop at Christmas, and that's a hard act to follow. So I feel kind of guilty about that kind of stuff. And I guess the reason I said I don't feel guilty is that I feel he's in good hands. But I also feel kind of sad that I can't do all those things. I think those things are worth doing. I want to bake at Christmas. It makes for a really nice, warm household. But I guess I'm just not ready yet.

Recommended Reading

Good Enough Mothers: Changing Expectations for Ourselves by Melinda M. Marshall. Peterson's, Princeton, NJ, 1993.

Working and Caring by T. Berry Brazelton. Addison-Wesley, Reading, Mass., 1992.

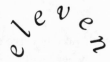

eleven

Ideal *During your maternity leave, you'll simply find a Mary Poppins or a well-situated, developmentally stimulating day-care center, and then you'll get right back to work.*

Fact *Finding day-care can be complicated and intimidating, and you usually have to work with what's available and affordable, not with what's ideal.*

Putting your baby in someone else's care is one of the hardest things you'll ever do, no matter what you think about day-care intellectually.

For one thing, once you have a flesh-and-blood infant—an infant who smiles at you as though you share her jokes, whose warm, soft head smells more delicious than any fragrance you've ever inhaled—the prospect of separation tends to loom more ominously than it did in or before pregnancy.

For another thing, the stories we hear about child care are usually horror stories. The evening news brings us shocking allegations of abuse and neglect, of rampaging psychopaths, and new "scientific" studies on the long-term psychological effects of "surrogate" care. Who does stories on warm, competent care givers who teach toddlers the alphabet and cuddle them after a fall?

Fortunately, the happy stories as well as the horror stories are true, but most real-life day-care is somewhere in the middle, with both good qualities and bad. However, there is no dependable standard of quality control, no definitive source that can tell you what kind of care to seek, where to find it, and how to be absolutely sure that what you've found will be good for the baby. Although your state probably regulates centers, and sitters who care for more than two or three children, the regulations focus on basic issues of safety and hygiene. No government inspector can tell you who's warm enough, smart enough, responsible enough, or disciplined enough for you—in short, which person or people you can trust to keep the baby safe and to communicate the sorts of values you'd like your child to absorb even when you're not there.

The first step in finding good child care is to sort out your priorities: What kind of care can you afford? What kind is tailored most closely to your working schedule? What kind will provide the kind of attention you feel your baby needs?

Paradoxically, you may not be able to answer all of these questions until you've already done some looking around. The form of care you *think* you'd like may not be readily available where you live, may cost more (in your neighborhood) than you can afford, or may turn out to have disadvantages you hadn't foreseen.

To help you get started, what follows is a general guide to the pros and cons of the three basic forms of child care: day-care centers, family day-care homes, and in-home help.

Day-Care Centers

The day-care center is one of the least expensive forms of child-care (unless you have a cooperative aunt or grandmother). It is also, in many ways, the most reliable. You know that your day-care center will be there the next morning, which is not always the case with the other two options. And you may also like the fact that your child will be exposed to lots of other children and adults from a very young age.

Of course, there are trade-offs. While you know the center will be open every day, you may not have the flexibility to pick your child up late on the days when work is crazy. If you're looking for part-time care, you may find it here only at full-time prices, if at all. You may feel that the baby wouldn't get enough individual attention, or would have to conform to institutional policies, like scheduled nap times, before he's old enough. Because the pay is usually low, many day-care centers have high staff turnover rates, which means that the child has to keep forming new attachments.

■ *How to Find Them.*   Many day-care centers don't take infants (babies under the age of two, or who haven't yet been toilet trained). Those that do often have waiting lists hundreds of names long. So if you're considering this form of care and have a deadline by which you know you'll need to return from a maternity leave, optimally you should have started making your phone calls during pregnancy to find out what's available in your area.

Day-care centers are easy to track down through the state agency that licenses them. If you find a center in any other way, check when you visit that a current, valid license is posted. But remember that a license indicates only that certain minimum standards of health and safety have been met. You still need to assess the facilities, the staff, the routine, the other children, and the general atmosphere in person.

If you expect the arrangement to be a long-term one, remember that you're assessing not just the center's infant care but its toddler program as well. And though you may not be ready yet with a list of questions about discipline and toilet training policies, just observing will teach you a great deal. If you visit late in the morning, for example, you might stay through the activities and lunch. Then you can see what sort of food is served, whether the staff sits with the children, and perhaps how staffers deal with a problem such as a child who doesn't like the meal.

The center should be able to give you a written copy of its regulations, which will include its policies on illness and vacations and other issues. If you have other questions—for example, what steps the center takes to protect the children against abuse—you shouldn't hesitate to ask the director. And really pay attention to the kind of answers you get; if you're not comfortable dealing with the director now, over theoretical issues, you're going to be in trouble later, when a real issue surfaces.

Old Wives' Tale: A Day-Care Center

Marsha has had her eighteen-month-old son at a day-care center since he was about three months old and she realized that the available home day-care in her neighborhood made her nervous.

I'd read all this stuff about how home day-care was supposed to be a better choice for infants. So I looked at a number of homes, both licensed and unlicensed. Most of the women seemed to be on welfare or had been on welfare and they didn't have very good safety standards and I didn't feel like I could relate to them.

Meanwhile, I'd heard about a day-care center that was opening in a hospital nearby. There were still spaces available (now, a year later, there's a waiting list of ninety children), so I lied and told them I was going back to work a month later than I was and asked them to hold his space open, because I was still thinking I *should* do home day-care.

I went ahead and put him in a home about three blocks away from me that I thought looked okay, even though the woman didn't even have plugs in her electrical outlets. Two weeks later, she announced that her grandmother had just died and she had to go to Oklahoma indefinitely. And I thought, "Forget this."

So I started taking him to the center. In the infant room, there were these wonderful grandmotherly ladies taking care of him. They gave me a lot of support, which was nice, since my mother isn't living. There were only six infants altogether. They let them sleep as much as they wanted, and whenever I was there and any of them was awake, they were holding them and playing with them. There were two care givers at all times, and if three of the babies were awake at the same time, the director would often come in and take the third.

I don't have total confidence in any one of the care givers in the toddler program, but I also feel that, since there are so many, what he can't get from one he can get from another. I like the exposure he's getting to other kids, learning to play with them and to share. And I think the center really reinforces the teaching I do about eating and brushing teeth.

They always call and let me know if he has a temperature, or if he falls—even when he seems perfectly okay, they call to tell me that he *did* fall but now he seems okay. Initially, they were going to have a sick bay, but they never got around to it. So if he has a temperature at 10:00 in the morning, I'm expected to come get him. But if he gets it at 3:00 in the afternoon, they might just say to pick him up when I finish work. When he's been so sick that they can't take him, I've taken him to another hospital that has a sick bay program for $3 an hour.

I still worry about the things every full-time working mother probably worries about. I worry about how my not being with him all day might be affecting him. There are many times I wish I could just spend the day there watching what he does. And I worry a little because I can't control all the influences on him.

For instance, sometimes he'll put his hands on his penis, which is fine with me. But then I noticed he's started feeling it and saying, "No, no, no!" So I think maybe someone at the day-care center told him, "No, no, no, you mustn't do that."

I don't like that, but I don't feel like I would be very effective at bringing that up with them. I think they'd just say, "Well, this is the way we do things." I don't know what would happen if I had a really serious disagreement with them, but so far, that hasn't come up. I wanted him to drink 2 percent milk, and the head of his room told me he couldn't unless I had a doctor's order. And I went to the director and said, "That's crazy. Are you going to tell me I really need to bother my doctor for this?" And she sort of laughed, but she said, "That's the way it is here." So I ended up having to get a note from the doctor saying he should drink 2 percent milk.

Financially, it's slightly more than family day-care would be, and considerably less than having someone come in. I paid $111 a week when he was an infant and I now pay $95 for the toddler program; it goes down because the older the children are, the more they can have for each care giver.

I don't worry about abuse. I can't imagine it. I suppose I should think about it, but he seems to happy, and the other kids seem happy. I guess it could happen anywhere, but I guess I feel his behavior would change if something weren't right. And he has gone through phases when he wants to cling to me when I drop him off. But most of the time, as soon as we pull up in the car, he's trying to get out of his car seat and in the doors, and he just walks right in and starts playing with the toys.

Family Day-Care

The second option is sending your child to be cared for in someone else's home. This arrangement can give you many of the benefits of institutional day-care and may be less expensive, depending on where you live. Most home day-care providers happily accept infants, and may be able to give them more individual attention than they'd get at a center (although that depends both on the adult-child ratios and the care giver's energy level). Home day-care allows the baby to be with other children—but not *too* many other children. It also keeps the baby in a homey atmosphere; some home day-care providers will take their charges out to parks and museums and libraries, just as you would if you were staying home. And home day-care providers *may* be more flexible than centers about certain child-care issues.

However, the quality of care can vary extraordinarily from

home to home. Licensing usually regulates factors such as how many children are allowed per adult care giver, how well child-proofed the houses is, and whether the care giver carries liability insurance. But it can't really guarantee you that she's the kind of person who remembers to put her aspirin away as soon as she takes it or keeps the front door locked at all times. If you go with an unlicensed provider (and the woman down the block who only looks after your baby in addition to her own, two days a week, doesn't need a license), you have no assurances whatever. In home day-care, unlike institutional care, the stability and judgment of the one care giver are paramount.

■ *How to Find It.* Finding a good family day-care home takes a mixture of persistence and good fortune. There's not much point in starting more than a few weeks before you need it, since most providers won't know about vacancies too far in advance and can't afford to hold an empty spot for too long.

You can start by calling the state agency that licenses home day-care providers. Although they can't recommend one home over another, they can give you a list of people who are licensed in your area, tell you what the standards are for licensing, and possibly refer you to other local organizations that can help you.

If you aren't working full-time, you might also consider unlicensed care; for example, a mother with one or two children of her own who doesn't want to commit herself to a full-blown family day-care business but is happy to have the extra income from a few days of sitting a week. This kind of arrangement tends to be less reliable than licensed care (the care giver may up and leave on a family vacation with a few days' notice, for example), but can also be more flexible, so that if, say, you need to work different days from week to week, you can keep renegotiating your schedule without having to pay for full-time care.

To find unlicensed care, you need to have good neighborhood contacts. Ask everyone you know or see with a baby if she knows of someone; if she uses someone herself, ask how she found the person. In some communities, there are certain classified sections or certain bulletin boards or certain organizations that everyone seems to rely on. You need to find out which those are. You may also want to call the state agency that licenses home day-care providers, just to find out what's required for licensing; then you can use their requirements as guidelines when you visit a prospective care giver's home.

Once you have a list, you need to call around to find out who has an opening and at what price. You also need to find out how long the person has been caring for children and whether she has references. (For more suggestions, see pages 211 and 212.) Assuming all this information checks out, you may want to chat a little more, telling her something about your baby's personality, asking about her background and why she decided to get into child care. If she sounds promising, ask if you can come meet her (while her charges are there if she's currently caring for anyone). If you're not sure, or turned off, tell her you have a long list of people to call and you don't want to schedule any appointments until you've talked to everyone. (If she sounds promising but has no opening, leave your name and phone number and ask her to call you if something does open up. Also ask her if she knows of anyone who's not on your list. And if, after a few weeks, you still haven't found an arrangement that satisfies you, call her back.)

For the visit, don't worry too much about lists of questions. Obviously, write down anything that occurs to you. But you may have to make a few visits and talk to a few people before you can even clarify what matters to you in a care giver. You should look around carefully to make sure that the house or apartment is child-proofed to your satisfaction. And you should ask to see everywhere the child will be allowed to go: backyards, basements, kitchens, and bathrooms. Also ask to see a license if you didn't find the care giver through the state agency (or, if you're too polite, you can call the agency afterwards to ask if she's licensed).

Most of all, watch the way the care giver interacts with your baby, with her own children, and/or with her charges. Try to have the kind of conversation with her you'd have with any mother you met in a supermarket checkout line; you'll learn more by asking her how she dealt with her own baby's night feedings than by asking about her abstract philosophy on dealing with a crying baby.

A licensed care giver will probably be able to give you a written list of rules regarding vacations and sick days and backup baby-sitters. Otherwise, once you've decided you really like someone, you need to try to establish as many ground rules as you can in advance. How much vacation does each of you get? How much do you pay her for? Do you pay her for days when your baby is sick? For days when she's sick? Does she have a backup sitter? How much notice will each of you give before ending the arrangement?

When you ask for references, try to get names of past clients as well as current ones. Sometimes parents gloss over problems with current day-care because they don't want to have to face up to them and force a confrontation or undertake the huge search for replacement care. Also, they may be afraid a negative comment will get back to the care-giver.

Old Wives' Tales

Finding Home Day-Care: "I looked at some pretty scary places."

Roxanne lived in a far-suburban area where home day-care wasn't easy to find. After two searches in less than a year, she had learned a lot about persistence, flexibility, and trust in her own judgment.

I was going back to work after a six-week maternity leave, and I thought what I wanted was someone coming in to take care of the baby. So I ran an ad in the local paper, which drew quite a few weirdos. Like a woman who wore reflective sunglasses and wouldn't take them off inside. She was the worst, but there were others who were almost as bad, who said things like, "I don't want to get a job where I have to clock in and out, so I thought I'd watch your kid."

So I started calling organizations involved in day-care, and they steered me toward some licensed day-care homes, which were all full. But the places that were full gave me more leads, and eventually, between all those calls and the calls to the people who answered my ad and the calls to friends who might know of someone, I easily spent $100 just on the phone bills.

I also looked at some pretty scary places. One woman seemed very nice, and her kids seemed happy, but in her kitchen there were dead bugs everywhere, even cooked onto the stove.

The one I decided on was relaxed, but not a slob. She was very warm, and she seemed like a person I could be friends with, who seemed to have similar values. But when I decided to cut down to part-time work, she said she needed full-time kids, and I had to look again.

The second time, it was much easier to look, because I had a better idea what I was doing. The new woman couldn't possibly get a license because her house is too crowded. But the kids are well cared for, and I like her, and the most important thing is that my daughter seems happy when I pick her up at night. I tried out another home before I found this one, and she was crying when I picked her up. The woman told me, "Kids are like that. She'll get over it in a couple of weeks." But I know my own daughter, and she's *not* like that. So I kept looking.

Finding Home Day-Care: "My instincts were right."

Nan lives in an apartment in a city and works part-time at home. Though she stumbled into home day-care, she quickly realized the situation is ideal for her.

When I started looking, at about two months, I was terrified of the whole idea. Even though I knew having the baby and a sitter in the apartment with me while I worked would be distracting, I was so scared to let the baby out of my sight that I felt I had to have someone come in. But I doubted I'd find someone flexible

enough to accommodate my needs. I didn't know how the business would go, or how much I'd be making, so I didn't know how
much time I'd need or could afford to pay for.

One of the women in my new-mother's group told me she knew
lots of people who'd found help through the local classified section,
so I put an ad in. Three of the people who called sounded decent.
Of those, one seemed in the interview to be a little off balance, and
the second, I think, might have been okay. The third was a graduate student's wife my age with a first baby my son's age, who lived
three blocks away from me. She was sweet and smart, and since I
couldn't see having *two* babies and an adult in the apartment with
me while I worked, I agreed to come over and look at her place. It
was bright and sunny and filled with plants and toys, and she and
her husband served us tea, and I was completely won over.

Even so, the first time I left him there, I came home and sat at
my desk and imagined that they belonged to some sort of white
slave ring and made plans about how I'd try to track them down
if I came back and the apartment was empty.

But my instincts were right. They were good, loving people,
who treated my son like one of the family, and he never showed the
slightest dismay over being dropped off there. Because she wasn't
sitting for anyone else, she was very flexible. I started out with two
four-hour afternoons a week and gradually increased to three seven-
hour days. And if I needed to get to a meeting on a day that wasn't
usually a sitting day, we would just switch the days around.

When the husband got his degree a year later, and they decided
to move away, the wife and I put our arms around each other and
sobbed.

In-Home Care

Generally speaking, this is the most expensive, most convenient, and least reliable option for child care. Its advantages are

clear: The baby gets to stay in her own home and doesn't have to share the caregiver's attention with anyone else. You don't have to get the baby up and bundled and off somewhere before getting to work yourself; if your help lives in, you don't even have to worry about her getting there on time. If your work requires late-night hours or overnight travel, a live-in is ideal, but a regular daytime sitter may also be willing to do the overtime. (A live-in, however, may be able to help with middle-of-the-night feedings and comforting.) And you may get some light housekeeping and cooking in the bargain.

On the other hand, daytime sitters are notoriously capable of failing to show up, and live-ins of threatening to quit with no notice (especially in sellers' markets such as New York City, where there have always been rumors of mothers stealing other mothers' sitters at the playground by offering fat raises). Trained nannies are extremely expensive, and if you can't afford that, then you can't count on the background in child development many day-care center workers have, or on firsthand mothering experience most home day-care providers have. And you may have to settle for someone who absolutely refuses to do any housekeeping or overtime.

Having someone in your home always entails a sacrifice of privacy. If you plan to work at home, you need Einsteinian powers of concentration or very well-insulated working quarters to accomplish anything while baby and sitter are in the house with you. And for a live-in, the more luxury you can afford in terms of separate living quarters, additional phone lines, and extra cars, the happier your prospects.

▪ *How to Find It.*   Starting with the grapevine is always prefer-
able. Ask other parents not only if they know of anyone who's
available but how they found their help, and whether they know
anyone else with in-home help. Your objective is to find out what
sources are commonly trusted in your area, whether they are pri-
vately run agencies, referral hotlines, or newspaper classifieds.

The first round of phone calls you make to potential sitters or
nannies are basic screening calls. You need to find out when the
person is available, what previous experience she has, and what
sort of pay she's looking for. You also need to give her some idea
of what your basic expectations are, so you don't waste time inter-
viewing someone who can't handle your regular Wednesday night
deadlines or who can't get to your house on her own or who's
allergic to your cat or whose cigarette smoke you're allergic to.
(For more suggested questions, see page 211.) Meanwhile, trust
the opinion you are forming from the way she responds, and
don't hesitate to put off someone who just doesn't *sound* right,
even if her answers are all technically okay. (If you're too polite to
do this directly, tell her you still have a long list of people to call
and you'll get back to her if you're interested.)

If you like the sound of her, go ahead and schedule an interview in your home. Assuming things go well, you should at some
point during the visit have her hold the baby, just to see how
comfortable she looks doing it and how comfortable you feel watching her. If she's a potential live-in, you should also show her the
accommodations you're offering.

If you're happy with the interview, the next step is to check
her references (see page 212). Before you definitely hire anyone,
be sure to work out an agreement about whether she'll get paid
for her (or the baby's) sick days, when your respective vacations
will be taken, and whether they'll be salaried. For a live-in nanny,
you may want to start with a trial day before she actually moves
in.

If you like the idea of an au pair from abroad, you might contact the American Institute for Foreign Study, which matches

American families in need of child care with young Europeans interested in spending time in this country. The au pairs, who range in age from 18 to 26, will work up to 45 hours a week in exchange for room, board, and fees totaling about $225 per week. (You'll also need to pay the au pair's airfare to your part of the country if you live outside the greater New York metropolitan area.) It takes from 6 to 12 weeks to find someone, and the baby must be at least three months old before being left alone in the house with the au pair.

For more information, contact the organization directly:

American Institute for Foreign Study
Au Pair Division
102 Greenwich Avenue
Greenwich, CT 06830
(203) 869-9090

Old Wives Tales

In-Home Care: "The tensions tend to build up"

Maureen lives in the city, in a small apartment, and works a forty-hour-plus week. Her life is full of stress, and she couldn't manage without the sitter; on the other hand, as she points out, the fifty-hour-a-week sitter adds another set of stresses.

We settled on our sitter because she seemed to have a lot of street-smarts, and to us, the number one concern in New York City is safety. There was another woman we actually liked much better, but she wanted a lot more money and she was willing to make only a year's commitment to the job, whereas ours said she was looking for three years.

Among the people I talk to, one year is about standard for a baby-sitter, because the tensions tend to build up and everyone wants a change. And now that we've had this one for a year, that's how we feel. There are a lot of problems we hadn't foreseen. She'd said when we interviewed her that she was willing to stay over when we went on business trips or on the occasional weekend vacation, but the first time we actually asked her to stay, she told us her husband wouldn't let her.

Also, she's expensive. We already pay her sixty-five dollars a day, and when we go out at night, we end up paying her an additional ten dollars an hour, when you figure in her cab fare.

And it bothers me that you don't really know what these sitters are doing all day. You can't know whether, when they take the kid to the park, they're really watching him or chatting with their friends. They hang out together all the time. They go shopping together; one of them will stand outside a store with all the carriages while all the others go in. We're not real happy about that.

So now we're thinking about getting a larger apartment and trying to find a live-in. That might solve our traveling problems, and I'd also like it if sometimes someone else could get up with him in the middle of the night, because sometimes I have to do it for days on end and then I'm a basket case at work.

In-Home Care: "You can't know until you try them."

Molly lives in a resort community, where she runs a bed-and-breakfast. Though not a new mother (her oldest child is 6), she's included here because over the past few years she has had a great deal of experience with live-in help—some of it fantastic, some of it horrific.

First of all, I'm very lucky. I only need the help during the tourist season, and at that point lots of college girls flock here looking for work. And I live in a big, rambling house, so I have room for live-in help. I guess even with a big house, some people would feel they were giving up privacy, but we were running a bed-and-breakfast and always had people around anyway, and my husband travels a lot, so I welcomed the company.

I had always managed to get someone. I'd offer free room and board in exchange for twenty hours a week of child care, and then the girl could get a part-time job waitressing or something for cash. It worked out fine.

Then one year, I put an ad in the paper and ended up hiring a twenty-seven-year-old woman who seemed very nice, very eager to live with us, and very good with the children. She had close friends nearby, and I called them as references and she checked out okay.

But as time went on, I started to realize that something was wrong. It became clear that the children didn't really like being with her, and that she had no idea how to handle that. But I was very busy, and I let things coast.

One day, she just completely broke down. I ended up chasing her all over town, with the cops out to help me, and shipping her off in a straitjacket. It turned out that she was a manic-depressive who'd thrown away all her medication. She'd been in various mental hospitals, which none of her references had told me, I guess because they thought she deserved a chance to prove herself. She hadn't done anything to the children, but still it was a nightmare, and for months I worried that she would try to come back.

My next live-in was no big success either. I had gotten the name of a woman in Ireland, and I called her up on the phone and spoke to her several times, and she said she was willing to come out here, so I flew her out. She lasted two weeks. She just wasn't willing to be flexible at all. We were living in a new house and opening a new hotel, and everyone just had to pitch in. She had a real chip on her shoulder, and you couldn't ask her to do anything. She'd come downstairs in the morning dressed in a suit and high heels, while I was in jeans and sneakers, as though she were the one going off to some executive job, while I was the baby-sitter. And her high heels ruined all my pine floors. And she'd have to have her cup of tea to start her day at 8:30, when all the rest of us had already been downstairs since 7:00. It just wasn't working out.

I ended up with a girl from Scotland, whom I'd met when she

worked in town the previous year. I called her up and asked if she wanted to come back and work for us, and she said yes. It worked out so well that we had her again the next summer, and then we had her sister, too. The only negative thing I can think of to say is that it was *so* painful whenever they had to leave. I paid them $150 a week, plus they got room and board and I paid their airfare.

My feeling is that, to some extent, it doesn't matter how much you interview these people, and how carefully you check their references. In the end, they either work out or they don't, and you can't know until you try them. But you really have to trust your instincts. If you feel like it's not working out, you can't just wait and hope it will get better, because it doesn't. It should work out instantly.

Other Child Care Arrangements

While day-care centers, family day-care homes, and in-home help are the three most common forms of child care, they aren't the only ones, or necessarily the best ones. Relatives, for instance, are a wonderful resource—if you have them nearby and they're willing to make the regular commitment. Otherwise, you may want to explore one of the following possibilities:

▪ *Sharing Someone Else's In-Home Help.* If you like the idea of lots of adult attention but also want to expose the baby early to other children, this situation may be ideal. Together, the two sets of parents can offer the care giver a higher wage than she'd get for just one baby; separately, they pay less than they'd have to pay for exclusive services.

The main drawback may be finding the sitter who feels she can handle two very young babies. Also, unless one family lives in a house with a yard, the care giver won't be able to get the kids outside unless you invest in or borrow a double stroller. And you become dependent on the other set of parents; if they pull out of the arrangement for any reason, you'll be left with the full financial burden until you can find another child.

To find potential partners, besides talking to people, you might try calling people who've run ads for in-home sitters, to ask if they're interested in sharing. Or run your own ad.

■ *Trading Time with Another Mother.*   If you free-lance or work part-time, this may be a great arrangement, because you'll never have to worry about your child-care costs. You also know (assuming that you've met and trust the other woman) that your baby is under a mother's care.

The big disadvantage here is the difficulty of finding another woman whose schedule dovetails nicely with your own. (You will almost certainly need to resort to bulletin boards and newspaper ads.) Also, your days off aren't really days *off*.

■ *Forming a Co-op.*   This is similar in theory to trading, but involves more people. For example, if four women who each need to work two days a week form a co-op, they can work out an arrangement by which each spends two days a week caring for the four babies, has two days to do other work while the other mothers sit, and one day completely off with her own child. In a modified arrangement, they might get together and hire a care giver, so that each mother would put in one day a week of sitting and get three days to herself. The four babies would always be watched by two people, one of them a mother. (If this sounds very complicated, see diagram on page 209.)

Obviously, the more people who get involved in this kind of arrangement, the more complicated it gets. Just finding the four people may be difficult. Then, if any one of them drops out, the whole schedule must be reworked. If you must count on being able to get somewhere on your working days, it probably wouldn't work. But if there's something creative you wouldn't have time for otherwise—if you want the time to write or paint, for instance—a co-op could be worth a try.

A co-op

	M	T	W	Th	F
4 mothers	M1, M2	M1, M3	M2, M4	M3, M4	Off
4 mothers + sitter	M1, sitter	M2, sitter	M3, sitter	M4, sitter	Off

When the Baby Is Sick

If you're using a day-care center or a family day-care home and your baby is too sick to go to it, the best arrangement is for you or your husband to stay home, or to get a friend or relative who's familiar to the baby. If that's not possible, however, there are two alternatives you might explore:

■ *Sick Bay Programs.* Some hospitals run special day-care programs for sick kids. To find one in an emergency, check the display ads under "Hospitals" in your yellow pages. However, the best strategy, if you know you have no backup sitters and will probably end up needing a program like this, is to call the hospitals in your area in advance and go visit any that run sick bays. That way, you won't be faced with the prospect of dropping a baby you're already worried about in a place you've never seen before. (In fact, many hospitals say they prefer to preregister children for sick bay programs so they'll have medical histories and other information on file in case of an emergency.)

Sometimes, in the case of a highly contagious disease such as chicken pox, even the hospital won't accept a child. Children it does accept will usually be grouped together in rooms according to their illness, so kids with stuffy noses don't end up catching something from the kids with upset stomachs.

Cost will vary from program to program, but may start as low as $3 an hour.

▪ *Temporary In-Home Care.* The other alternative is to get a temporary caregiver to come to your home, preferably a nurse. You can find agencies that specialize in this service through the yellow pages, under "Nurses," or through a day-care referral agency or hotline. This is an especially good arrangement if both you and the baby are sick.

Don't be afraid to ask lots of questions on the phone. Definitely ask how the agency finds its people, what kind of experience they have, how long they stay with the agency, and whether the agency has actually spoken to their references about them. Also ask if the agency itself has references—people who've used its services whom you could talk to.

Basic Sources for Child-Care Information

In addition to the agencey in your state that licenses daycare providers, here are some other places to call.

▪ The National Association for the Education of Young Children (NAEYC): 1-800-424-2640. Tell them where you live, and they'll put you in touch with resource and referral organizations in your area. They'll also send you a brochure called "How to Choose a Good Early Childhood Program."
▪ Child Care Aware: 1-800-424-2246. Sponsored by Dayton Hudson and a group of national and local child-care quality advocates, Child Care Aware aims both to train good providers and to help parents identify good care. Again, they can give you numbers of your local referral organizations.
▪ Your local chamber of commerce. Sometimes they maintain lists of licensed child-care programs.

Family Day-Care and In-Home Day-Care:
Basic Screening Questions

You can save a lot of time screening potential sitters on the phone if you're able to come up with a list of requirements that matter to you. What follows is a basic, generic list to start you off. Revise it as you clarify your own priorities.

Name
Phone number
When available to start
Previous experience
References
Smoker or not
What days available (any flexibility from day to day?)
What length of commitment expected (just summer? until finished with school?)
Expected pay or fee

For family day-care providers:
Licensed by the state? (First, find out from your state what the requirements are)
Where located
How many other kids and what ages
How many other adult care givers, if any

For in-home care givers:
Have driver's license and own transportation
Could come by public transportation
Willing to do housekeeping
Willing to cook
Willing to stay some evenings and weekends (and at what rate)

Basic Questions for References

Don't accept a name or a written reference at face value; always call the reference and ask for more information. You could just ask, "What did you think of her?" but sometimes you need to be a little more aggressive in priming the pump. Some suggestions:

"How long have you known her? How did you find her?"
"Why did you stop using her?" (If applicable)
"What do/did you like best about her?" (Follow up. If reference says, "She's very responsible," ask for examples of what she did responsibly.)
"Did anything ever happen while your child was in her care that upset or worried you?"
"Would you use her again?"

For home day-care providers:
"Was your child happy when dropped off and picked up?"
"Was the house clean and safe?"

For in-home care givers:
"Did she do housework? If so, how well?"
(For daily sitter): "Was she prompt?"
(For live-in sitter): "What did she do in her off-duty time?"

For both:
"Is there anything else about her you think is important that I haven't asked about?"

A P.S. about references: Remember that references aren't infallible. They may not tell you everything they know, and they may not know everything there is to know. By the same token, if a candidate who appeals to you very strongly doesn't, for some sensible reason, have any references, you may want to take the risk. Above all, trust your instincts.

twelve

Ideal *There is such a thing as a Good Mother, and if you try hard enough and make all the right choices, you can be one.*

Fact *It is possible to be a good mother—if by "good" you don't really mean "perfect," which many women do. This chapter takes a closer look at where our images of ideal mothers come from: Mythical Mothers, Memory Mothers, and Media Mothers.*

If you've read through most of this book—particularly the material in chapter 5 on the history of child-care advice and in chapter 10 on the history of women's work—it should be clear that society's expectations of what a mother should be and do have shifted during the past few centuries. And perhaps the most drastic of these changes has occurred in the past twenty years, since the wide availability of dependable birth control and legal abortion have made motherhood a woman's option rather than her fate.

Today it is virtually impossible to have a baby without at some point asking yourself, "*Should* I become a mother?" And a close corollary of that question is, "What kind of mother do I want to be?" You may wrestle with this question on a grand scale if you find yourself agonizing over whether to stay on at your job or quit, for example. But even if you never have to sit down and make an actual decision about your philosophy, you're likely to find the question cropping up again in subtle ways during early motherhood. Do you want to be just like your own mother, or nothing like her?

My mother did a lot of things I didn't want to do. There was a lot of saying, "If you do this, something bad will happen to you." I was lied to, not because they were bad parents, but because they didn't know how to handle certain situations. I still remember when I had to go into the hospital to have an operation, and my mother told me I was going to have my picture taken, and the next thing I knew they were putting a gas mask over my face and I was scared out of my wits. I was six years old, and it's still sticking with me.

Do you expect the baby to fit more or less into your life and your schedule, or do you see yourself primarily as a facilitator of the baby's growth and development?

I want to make sure that he's always being stimulated. We have many different playthings, as you can see, and I'll move him around from one to another. I don't like to just drop him somewhere. I have a friend who had a baby at the same time as I did, and she just puts him in the swing and lets him swing all day long. He has a bald spot in the back of his head where it touches the swing.

Do you expect to raise the child according to the religious and cultural mores you yourself grew up with, or do you hope to raise a child who'll help change the world?

I want Gus to be a different kind of male. I want him to be his own person, but I want to filter what the patriarchy will try to make him be. I want him to balance what he sees in the world with images of lots of competent, caring, fun, athletic, working women.

The kind of mother we all want to be, of course, is a Good Mother. The trouble is, nobody quite knows what that means anymore. In a world where psychoanalysts can unlock our deepest fears and resentments, who knows whether our own mothers were good or bad? In a world where we see TV reports on two-year-olds learning to read and then read articles about "hurried" children suffering from burnout and depression, who knows how much stimulating helps a kid compete? In a world where one generation's *All in the Family* (about a conservative couple and their hippie-liberal kids) is another's *Family Ties* (about a hippie-liberal couple and their yuppie-conservative kids), who can say what politics our mothering will produce?

And amidst the uncertainty, it is easier to feel like a bad mother than a good one. We have little impressive documentation on how anyone's mother helped them to become a healthy, well-adjusted, productive citizen, but we do know beyond a shadow of doubt that, for example, in *Psycho*, Norman Bates's mother flipped him out, that the Manchurian Candidate's mother manipulated him, and that Portnoy's mother made him complain. And from our own experience we learn quickly that we can't always stop our infants from crying, that we lose our temper more easily than we wish we would, that our children go ahead and get bruised and cut and sick no matter how hard we try to watch and protect them.

In other words, it's quite easy for any of us to make long lists of the ways in which mothers may fail or be inadequate. But anyone who isn't perfect sometimes fails or is inadequate. So where did we get our ideas about how perfect a mother should be? To what standard, exactly, are those of us who strive to be "good" mothers trying to hold ourselves? Where, in short, do we get our images and ideas of good mothering from?

Mythic Mothers

We look first to mythology, folklore, and religion, for these are the earliest media through which ancient images of mothers and motherhood have been preserved and transmitted in forms that still shape our lives today. And one of the very oldest stories in what might loosely be called the Greco-Roman-Judeo-Christian tradition is the Greek myth of Demeter and Persephone, which goes like this:

Demeter was the goddess of the harvest. Hades, the god of the underworld, fell in love with her daughter, Persephone, and carried her off one day as she gathered flowers in a field. Demeter was inconsolable. She wandered the earth in search of her daughter and finally, in despair, cursed the soil which seemed to have swallowed her up. Because of the curse, the crops failed and cattle died and all life was threatened.

Finally, a witness described the abduction to her, and Demeter pleaded with Zeus, the father of all gods and men, to force Hades to return Persephone. Zeus agreed, on the condition that Persephone hadn't eaten anything while in the underworld. Hades accepted the agreement, but meanwhile offered Persephone a pomegranate, of which she ate several seeds. So, although she was allowed to rejoin her mother, for half of each year she was forced to return to Hades as queen of the underworld.

The myth is usually regarded as an allegory of agriculture: Persephone represents the crops, which spend half the year growing and then nourish human life, but which for half the year shrivel, die, and disappear, leaving the earth barren. Feminists embrace the story; not only is it one of the few in *any* tradition in which a woman acts, out of love, to save another woman from unwanted possession by a man (and a king, to boot) but it also recalls a time in which the unique and fundamental power of women to create and nurture life was recognized and celebrated by society. And it is no mere fireside tale; for thousands of years, the Greeks annually processed from Athens to Eleusis to worship at Demeter's shrine and celebrate her mysterious powers.

But in most of the Greek and Roman myths, it is male life and achievement which is celebrated. Feminist historians speculate that, as agriculture came to be somewhat less mysterious, and warfare a stronger determinant of political and economic success, the values of the society—preserved in the myths—shifted to "male" attributes. Thus we have the tales of heroes, young males who break away from the childhood world of their mothers, undergo trials and perform feats of strength and daring, and when fully tested are finally recognized as men.

Meanwhile, the capacity of women to be strong and nurturing seemed to dwindle, replaced in mythology by an increasingly misogynistic, schizophrenic view of them either as ideal, untouchable, and virginal, or earthy, seductive, and corrupting. So the Greek myth of Pandora, in which the first woman, created by the gods for man's pleasure, disobediently opens a box and releases a multitude of plagues upon mankind, is clearly and even more ferociously echoed in the biblical story of Adam and Eve. Here Eve is specifically told that her punishment for disobedience will include "sorrow" in bringing forth children. Thus begins a Jewish-Christian notion that whatever pain women suffer in childbirth and motherhood has been called down upon them by their own inadequacies.

The paradigm of motherhood passed down to us from Christianity is, of course, Mary, mother of Christ. But Mary, despite her motherhood, fits more neatly into the tradition of the idealized virgin. She is known as the mother of Christ; he, however, is known as the son of God. It is God's creativity which is worshiped here, not the creativity of woman's flesh. It is not her power (and certainly not her sexuality) which is glorified, but her submissiveness, both to God's will and her son's fate. She is as far along the spectrum from Demeter's voracious, earth-destroying passion as can be. She is the correction of those "weaknesses" said to have crippled Pandora and Eve, and through them, all humanity. We see her, through artists' renderings, serenely at one with her child, held to her breast. She is the perfect mother, for unlike Demeter, Pandora, and Eve, who tried to satisfy their own emotional and intellectual needs, Mary is utterly at her child's disposal.

Memory Mothers

Psychologists have offered a very different interpretation of where myths about powerful women, about ideal and evil mothers, come from. Instead of representing an actual, historical shift in social and political conditions (i.e., from a time in which women were powerful and worshiped to a time in which they were subjugated by men), many psychologists—including Freud and Jung—have argued that such myths spring from a universal stage of individual psychological development. This is the preverbal stage of infancy, during which almost all babies are under the exclusive care of women. The powerful mother of myth therefore represents our own mother, at a time when she really did hold the power of life and death over us. The tendency of myth to portray women either as unrealistically beautiful and good or as hopelessly evil and ugly represents an ambivalence as old as civilization itself about our earliest total dependence on our mothers.

Why should this ambivalence be so universal? It may help to take a quick layperson's look at the Oedipal complex, Freud's theory (named for a character in Greek mythology) of how boys develop their sexual identities and, to a great extent, their selfhood.

Very simply, both boys and girls feel their earliest passionate attachment to their mothers, the sources in infancy of warmth, nourishment, and comfort. A boy's first sexual feelings are also for his mother, but they are accompanied by the anxious sense that should his father guess at the rivalry, his father would castrate him. The boy resolves this fear by giving up his love for his mother and identifying with his father. In the process, he gives up "childish" things: the ways of his woman-dominated domestic youth, with all its easy dependence, its spontaneous affection and perfect trust. Instead he adopts the ways of outside, male culture: independence, competitiveness, self-control, achievement. His sense of mastery in this man's world satisfies his residual infant's panic at not having all his needs instantly fulfilled.

Thus, happy childhood or no, it makes sense that the man should remain ambivalent throughout his life in his attitude toward women/mothers. On the one hand, he recalls at some level the infant's perfect security and bliss in the all-powerful mother's arms; but, on the other hand, his subconscious mind also recalls the rage of not having always been satisfied, and he must resist the temptation of seductive infantile dependence if he is to continue successfully in his father's world.

Projected into the stories men tell, the myths handed down across centuries, the evil mother thus does not represent wrongs done by a real mother in childhood; she may actually represent the man's fear of falling under the power of someone who once seemed so powerful and now seems so inadequate to safeguard him in his real world. An ideal mother, by the same token, would be one who could fulfill all of his adult needs just as some powerful woman once fulfilled his infant needs. And this is just what the fairies and goddesses of mythology usually do.

Such a theory is very useful in helping us understand both our own feelings about mothers and why psychology's attempts to describe motherhood have been, to date, so woefully inadequate. Quite simply, all of us—myth makers and bards, mothers-to-be and new mothers, psychologists and researchers—regard our own mothers and the idea of motherhood with a volatile and irrational mixture of idealism and resentment. And this child's-eye view of mothers permeates psychological theory as thoroughly as it does mythology. Just as in mythology there are few gradations between the beautiful virgins and the wicked witches, so in the psychological literature there isn't much gray area in between the good mothers and the bad ones. The bad ones, of course, are those who, by neglecting their children's needs, cripple them for life with neuroses and anxieties. The good ones are almost never drawn from real-life examples. The Good Mother is a theoretical construct whose characteristics are extrapolated by contrast to the Bad Mother's. Presumably, she is completely sensitive to her children's needs and always free to devote herself to meeting them. However, she is not to be confused with the form of Bad Mother, also popular in the literature, who by anxiously anticipating all the child's needs thereby smothers him, crippling him for life with neuroses and anxieties.

In other words, mainstream psychology has always defined motherhood from the child's point of view. And, having defined her duties and obligations this way, it has jumped right to the assumption that "normal" mothers would be totally fulfilled by meeting these obligations. As Freud formulated it, the little girl solves her version of the Oedipal complex by becoming her mother; presumably, she compensates for her rage at unmet infantile needs by becoming the all-powerful mother figure, and thus doesn't need mastery of the male, achievement-oriented world.

Or, as Dr. John Bowlby, who formulated the concept of "maternal deprivation," put it in the 1950s, "The provision of constant attention night and day, seven days a week and 365 days in the year, is possible only for a woman who derives profound satisfaction from seeing her child grow from babyhood, through the many phases of childhood, to become an independent man or woman, and knows that it is her care which has made this possible."*

Psychology, therefore, has defined the ideal mother exactly as an infant might—as one who can provide "constant attention day and night, seven days a week and 365 in the year"—and defined as normal one who derives from this constant responsibility "profound satisfaction." But suppose that instead of leaving the definition of "normal" mothers to men, who, after all, have only been sons, we gave it to women, who have had the chance to understand both the child's and the mother's point of view?

For the most part, psychologists have been male, and when confronted with questions about female behavior have made one of two assumptions about it—either that it was identical to male behavior (in the way the pronoun "he" is said to represent both men and women), or, in cases where it has seemed obviously

* John Bowlby, *Child Care and the Growth of Love*, pp. 79–80.

different, that it was abnormal, inadequate, or weak. Thus, for example, Freud saw women's desire to have children as springing from their profound sense of castration; since they could not have penises, like men, they would fill their wombs with babies.

In our day, the idea of penis envy seems quaint and silly. If anyone's envious, feminists have argued, it's more likely to be men, who have no miraculous capacity to form and nourish new human beings from their own flesh. Yet metaphorically, if a penis is presumed to symbolize all those things men have but to which women have traditionally been denied access, the whole feminist movement of the 1970s could be seen as a massive outpouring of penis envy. "No," women said, "we no longer believe full wombs and lots of babies are substitutes for what your penises have always entitled you to: money, power, independence, a voice."

In the initial thrill of liberation, it seemed obvious that if women wanted so badly what men had, then what men had and the way they had to get it was, as Freud had said, right and normal. What women had traditionally had—lives based on nurturing relationships—was clearly weaker. The pronoun "he" was truly universal. Everyone, male or female, could accept the model of the mythic hero and his quest as an androgynous metaphor for how human beings achieve "selfhood."

More recently, much feminist thought has been tempered by an awareness that most women can't, happily, model their lives on men's. Carol Gilligan's ground-breaking 1981 book *In a Different Voice* set forth a theory that women's psychology was neither identical to men's nor a sort of stunted version, but was quite clearly different; only because women function in a world whose moral, ethical, political, economic, and of course, psychological standards are determined by men are women's differences usually defined as weaknesses.

Along those lines, Kathryn Allen Rabuzzi's 1988 book *Motherself* pointed out that the hero's quest is not, in fact, an accurate metaphor for the way women achieve selfhood—or, more specifically, for the way women cope with the changes in their self-hood that normally occur if and when they become mothers. If anything, a woman becoming a mother must learn to shrug off some of the heroic principles she has embraced in order to compete in a man's world. Whereas the hero achieves mastery by exerting physical control over monsters and dragons, the woman must submit to the losses of control over her physical self which occur with pregnancy and labor. (The reverberations of this essential male/female difference can be heard in the complaints of feminists and natural childbirth enthusiasts that the whole history of medical intervention in childbirth is actually the story of man's attempt to seize control of childbirth from women. Midwives, the women who have historically attended laboring women, are much less likely to interfere with the natural course of labor by using drugs or high-tech equipment. However, even feminists and natural childbirth enthusiasts tend to advocate such techniques of pain "control" as Lamaze or Dick-Read breathing. As we noted in chapter 1, controlling oneself in labor may actually hurt women more than it helps them.) Similarly, whereas the hero must learn to cultivate his self-sufficiency and to pursue his heart's desire at all costs (or, as Joseph Campbell phrased it, to follow his "bliss"), a woman becoming a mother must develop her capacity to sense the unspoken needs of the baby and to subordinate her own desires to meeting those needs, as nursing mothers quickly discover. (And again, this male/female difference may throw some light on the fact that so much of the child-care advice that has to do with imposing the parents' will on the baby—feeding schedules, separate beds and rigid bedtimes, avoidance of too much holding and "spoiling" of infants—often seems to have originated with men and doesn't, for most women, work.)

The fact is that most women today have to learn both models of selfhood. They cannot simply become mothers, in the sense that Freud thought this constituted an identity. They are too likely to need the second income to keep the family going, to earn the primary income if the marriage disintegrates, or to be the sole support of a family that has no adult male contributor. And even if her material needs are taken care of, a woman with two or three children isn't likely to be occupied full-time with their care for more than ten to fifteen years; that leaves her with about thirty adult, pre-retirement-age years in which she'll need to find something else to occupy her attention.

Nor can women simply become like their fathers, if they decide to have children. Even many men of our generation are beginning to recognize that the role their fathers played in parenting was sadly inadequate. And many a smart, talented, ambitious woman is coming to realize that the rules under which male management expects her to succeed don't allow for the schedules, sicknesses, and silly whims of little children.

A balanced view of "good" motherhood would take into account both the child's needs and the mother's. A mother who enjoyed spending most of her time with her young children and who could afford to do so would do so, without judging herself in "hero" terms for the duration. A woman who needed work, either for the money or for the intellectual stimulation, would satisfy herself that her child care was competent and reasonably affectionate and then ignore the media pronouncements of "experts" who don't know a thing about her circumstances, her personality, or her values.

One point to keep in mind, even as you try to speculate about how your children will judge the job you did at mothering, is that no one has ever proved or will ever prove that having all needs met *by the mother* is possible or even desirable. In the words of Ann Dally, author of *Inventing Motherhood*:

> Today there is much talk in child care circles about "bonding," the affective ties that develop between an infant and whoever cares for him. These bonds are known to be of profound importance in development. As a result, some people behave as though bonding was the *only* aspect of childhood that matters. This narrow view deriving from Bowlby and still

more from his followers has led not only to greater understanding of children but also to ignoring on a vast scale their other needs. These include the need for stimulation and opportunities for play, variety of experience and a stable, happy mother with the opportunity to be a mother in the way that best benefits her and her children. It also ignores the enormous variation in personality among mothers, many of whom are capable of being good mothers, but not if they have to mother [24 hours a day, 365 days a year]. *

But the last word on the psychology of motherhood goes to Sheila Kitzinger, a social anthropologist who has written extensively about birth and mothering:

> Learning how to be a mother is not a matter of adopting a certain set of attitudes, but of expressing one's own personality in the task of responding flexibly to the child's needs. Each woman brings a unique combination of skills and experience to motherhood. There is no such thing as the "perfect" mother, if only because the role only achieves meaning when it is part of a growing dyadic relationship with a child, and if there are other children in the family, the relationship between all the children and their mother, and between each and every combination of them. The mother sees herself in their eyes, as she must do also in the eyes of her husband. What she is and the way she conceptualizes her own role is to a large degree a product of all these images of the self, which, especially in a large family, in each day and every hour of each day are subjected to kaleidoscopic transmutations, depending on the situation and the actors.
>
> Motherhood is, in fact, never really learned. It evolves.†

* Ann Dally, *Inventing Motherhood: The Consequences of an Ideal.* Schocken Books, New York, 1983, p. 89.

† Sheila Kitzinger, *Women As Mothers: How They See Themselves in Different Cultures.* Vintage Books, New York, 1980, p. 178.

Media Mothers

In this era of mass communications, all of us have to cope daily with the powerful images of strangers which are transmitted into our lives by TV, radio, newspapers, movies, books, and magazines. It is from these sources that the myths of our own time emerge: stories and ideas containing some grain of truth or fact, but largely embellished by our own fears and fantasies.

"Media images of mothers" is an enormous, unwieldy subject encompassing everything from women's suffrage to the ERA, from Rosie the Riveter to Betty Crocker to Betty Friedan to Roseanne. In this book, I've chosen to look at only the prevailing current model, Celebrity Moms, as portrayed for us by popular magazines. These are the ultimate working mothers—the women who seem to have accomplished what we dream of accomplishing, who give form and definition to the great myth of our own time: Having It All. We have a love-hate relationship with them. Smiling gorgeously at us from the magazine's pages—cosmetically and perhaps surgically enhanced, their household help and personal trainers nowhere to be seen—they set an apparent standard for success that none of us women with average-or-below incomes or looks can possibly hope to achieve. Yet certainly over the course of the past two decades, their widely publicized escapades have helped diversify and expand the public conception of what motherhood entails—apart from 24-hour vigilance in the nursery. The very ubiquity of the celebrity profile suggests that, no matter how much larger-than-life their resources or domestic arrangements, we persist in believing we can learn something from the details of these people's lives. Can we? Well, let's try.

Q: Who are America's best-known Celebrity Moms?
A: As the second edition of this book goes to press, America's newest and best-known Celebrity Mom is Madonna, who managed to make the transition from in-your-face sex symbol to be-

nign beatific *Redbook* covermom in under a year. And despite her long and passionate career as the self-appointed Challenger of Bourgeois Sexual Mores, she has suddenly begun dispensing suspiciously Yuppie-sounding child-rearing advice. No electronic babysitter for Lourdes, the media queen told *Redbook.* "*TV's* poison."

In fact, after spending the Eighties obsessed with the question of whether women in dress-for-success suits and full-time jobs were also suitable for mothering (Jane Pauley was a favorite symbol of these women, even though most working women—including the ones in the suits—weren't earning six-figure salaries and riding around in network chauffered cars), magazines in the Nineties have been preoccupied with the question of whether women who have high-profile sexuality can be suitable mothers. Actress Demi Moore seems to have ignited this controversy by posing naked and huge-bellied with her second daughter for the cover of *Vanity Fair* in 1991. She claimed to be challenging a stereotype by confronting people who "don't want to embrace motherhood and sensuality" because they are "afraid to imagine a pregnant woman as sexy" (Interview, July 1996). And while a lot of us were indeed convinced that Demi Moore, at least, could pull off being pregnant and sexy, it wasn't clear that she'd done the average childbearing woman any big favors. Ditto a year later, when she reappeared on the cover in her now infamous bodypaint-only costume, and in an inside photo spread designed to "unveil her new figure." Boy-hipped and flat-bellied, the New Figure was supposed to have resulted from hours of daily workout with a personal trainer, and certainly did nothing to bolster the sexual self-image of any nanny-less, cook-less, cleaning-help-less new mother who'd spent her first few post-partum months wondering if she'd *ever* have another hour free to exercise.

Another surprising Nineties covermom, or mom-to-be at the time, was rock star Melissa Etheridge, who appeared on the cover of *Newsweek* in November of 1996 with "her pregnant partner, Julie Cypher." In her case, the magazine posed the question of whether her high-profile homosexuality (or, for that matter, the lower-profile homosexuality of thousands of non-famous lesbians) rendered her suitable for motherhood. Ultimately, the article concluded, "it is the quality of the parenting—not the parents' lifestyle—that matters most to kids. Sexual orientation alone doesn't make a person good or bad."

Certainly, heterosexuality has not guaranteed parental stability, even to Celeb Moms, over the years. Of the nine Celeb Moms cited in this book's first edition—all of whom were said at the time to Have It All, including true love—only three were still married to the same man seven years later.*

Q: What about Celeb Dads?
A: Although some of the more traditional Celeb Moms—Katie Couric, for example, and Maria Shriver—are married, there has been a recent trend away from having an actual legal attachment to the sperm donor. Madonna, naturally, is in the avant garde. She confided to *Redbook*, "I can think of all sorts of people who are married who have perfectly revolting relationships and terribly unhealthy relationships. I don't think marriage is a guarantee of anything" (Jan 1997). Melissa Etheridge and Julie Cypher declined to tell *Newsweek* who their sperm donor was, but when asked, "What about the father's role? Isn't that an important part of raising a child?" they replied noncommittally, "We will have male figures" (Nov 4, 1996). Actresses Diane Keaton, Kate Jackson, and Rosie O'Donnell adopted as single parents. Robin Wright had two children with Sean Penn *before* they eventually married.

However, if single Celeb Moms don't seem to consider Mr. Celebs indispensable, those Mr. Celebs who are in residence are, without exception, always anointed Superdads. Katie Couric says her husband, Jay Monahan, who left a high-powered Washington law firm to join her in New York after their first child was born, is "the most involved father, and he does it cheerfully. He doesn't

---

* Jane Pauley, Meryl Streep, and Demi Moore are still married at this writing. Cybill Shepherd, Christie Brinkley, Danielle Steel, Princess Diana, and Sarah Ferguson have all been divorced at least once. Princess Caroline of Monaco has been widowed.

act like he's doing me a big favor." She says he got up with the baby in the middle of the night (presumably on weekends, when the live-in sitter wasn't there) and always gets the older one up and ready for school while Katie's on the set of "Today."

Arnold Schwarzenegger told *McCall's* in January of 1997, "I am a father first, an actor second." He says he wouldn't let his kids, aged 7, 5 and 3, see any of his action films because "They are too young and the movies are too violent." (For the record, Madonna says she doesn't want Lourdes perusing *Sex* either.) This might explain Schwartzenegger's compulsion to make films like *Kindergarten Cop* and *Jingle All the Way*.

Bruce Willis, less concerned than his wife about the possible chilling effects of parenthood on his sex appeal, was quoted in *Time* in 1995 as saying, "I change diapers. I clean up dog doo. I take the trash out, and I wash clothes. Some days I'm Mr. Mom. A few years ago I was out there partying. Now a happening night is acting out all the roles from *The Wizard of Oz* for my kids."

Even Michael Jackson has snatched at the grace-conferring mantle of high-profile fatherhood. After initially proclaiming that he would not allow first-born son Prince to grow up "in a fish-bowl," as he himself had, Jackson allowed Britain's *OK!* magazine to pay him $2 million for the first authorized photos of himself and the infant. "I'm in bliss 24 hours a day," he assured the magazine's reporter, and mother Debbie Rowe avowed that "He loves being involved in every aspect of caring for the baby . . . feeding him, holding him and, of course, singing to him."

Q: But don't Celeb Moms and Dads have lots of hired help to take care of things like feedings and diaper-changes and cleaning up the dog doo?
A: Well, actually they *do* have quite a bit of help, but *sssssh!* It is a universal convention of the Celeb profile that having roughly the same number of servants as a feudal European estate *must never be alluded to.*

Thus, for example, *People's* April 21, 1997 glorious seven-page full-color spread on actress Jane Seymour's "Malibu Dream House" painted a 99% help-free portrait of the Celeb Mom's cozy home life with her third husband, four resident children, and frequently in-for-supper in-laws. The immaculate and gleaming appearance of the 11,000 square-foot, mostly beige and white, three-level sandstone house was apparently due to the fact that the family "never wears shoes" inside. Husband Stacey Keach had *personally* supervised the house's extensive renovation, "a move his business manager estimates may have saved $1 million in construction misunderstandings." He also *personally* designed the "extensive gardens," Koi ponds, and swimming pool—from which he *personally* pumped water during some California brushfires, "saving five houses on the bluff." The backyard beach, tennis and basketball courts, screening room, art studio, putting green, and Rollerblading path appear to be self-maintaining. And when 16-month-old twins Kristopher and John need a bath, Seymour and her 11-year-old son Sean *personally* don swimsuits and take them into the master bath Jacuzzi. "It's the only way," Jane asserts, to "manage the naked boys. They wriggle a lot."

There *is* one passing reference to a housekeeper, to whom Seymour, "to save time, taught . . . her favorite recipes." Still, the family apparently does without this woman each weekend and stoically faces the consequences: "We order in," says Seymour, "or you starve."

(Incidentally, according to the same *People* article, the Seymour-Keach clan also spends several weeks a year at its other house, which actually happens to *be* a feudal European estate; or, more specifically, a 1,000-year-old restored monastery in Bath, England.)

Q: Do Celeb Moms have trouble reconciling the responsibilities of motherhood with the demands of their careers?
A: Not nearly as much as they did in the Eighties. They used to have to try to hide their pregnancies for as long as possible and

stow the kids at home with nannies while they were filming. But the Hollywood studio has apparently become extremely baby-friendly in recent years. Jane Seymour reported that when she suffered overwhelming nausea while pregnant with the twins, the staff at "Dr. Quinn, Medicine Woman" was very accommodating: "Every time I walked onto the Dr. Quinn set, they'd hand me a bucket." In November 1996 she told *People* that not only did she bring the then-11-month-old twins to work with her, but her co-workers were deeply grateful to her for doing this. "When people [on the staff] get stressed out, they'll ask my permission to take a baby for a walk and come back and say, 'Thank you! I feel much better now.'"

Demi Moore, whom *McCalls* (March 1996) characterized as a "surprisingly hands-on mother," lets her three daughters "spend a great deal of time on her movie sets and in the offices of her production company, and she gives them occasional acting parts." Her youngest, Tallulah Belle, played her baby in The Scarlet Letter, while her oldest, Rumer, played her daughter in Striptease.

(That *McCalls* profile, by the way, was one of the very few Celeb Mom pieces to note the existence of "what has been described as an entourage of assistants, chauffeurs, housekeepers, cooks, massage therapists, . . . bodyguards," and of course, nannies surrounding Moore and Willis in all their many homes and work-places.)

Q: *If they really do Have It All, then is there anything Celeb Moms worry about?*
A: Sure. They agonize over the probability that their children will get all messed up by growing up Having It All. They'd do anything to make sure their kids could have a Normal Childhood, as yours will.

Katie Couric: "I don't want [her daughter] to be an elitist snob who focuses on material things and thinks that people should get BMWs for their sixteenth birthday" (Good Housekeeping, Aug 1996).

Roseanne to the *Ladies Home Journal* in June 1996, after the birth of her fifth child: "I want to quit Hollywood, because I don't care about any of it. All I want to do now is be a housewife."

Madonna: "It's really important for my daughter to be around other kids. But I don't want her to go to school with a bunch of rich kids. And I don't want her to go to an all-white school."

Q: So are Celeb Moms really happy?
A: Yes, absolutely. Because we've come full circle, from an age in which any woman could be a mom but few could go out and succeed on their own terms, to an age when, apparently, any old woman can become a Celeb, but not all are blessed with the ultimate Hollywood Happy Perk.

As the inimitable Roseanne so compassionately put it, illustrating how the joy of motherhood has overflowed into every area of her life, even mellowing her attitude toward "rival female TV superpower Oprah Winfrey": "I pity her in a way. She doesn't have any kids."

Old Wives' Tales

"I Want Her to Grow Up and Have All These Options I Don't Think I Have."

Wendy, twenty-eight, is a full-time mother largely by choice, but she is haunted by what she sees as a Catch 22: the responsibility she feels to her baby keeps her from taking the time to discover a career that might make her happy; yet she also considers it her responsibility as a Good Mother to raise her daughter in such a way that the girl will have some destiny more exciting than full-time motherhood.

I wasn't raised competitively at all; intellectually and socially, I was sort of a nerd, but that was okay because I had four older brothers looking out for me, and they took care of me. I guess I was very much protected, and I never had to put myself on the line. For a few years before I got pregnant, I started to act as a hobby. And it turned out I wasn't bad at it, and people started suggesting that I do it seriously. So, as soon as I got that idea in my head, I froze. I got horrible stage fright. I couldn't make myself go to auditions.

I never finished school, and I never really found a career before I got pregnant, just a bunch of different jobs. I've thought about going back to work now, but I've realized there's no business I could possibly care about as much as I care about her. Why should I care about how much money some company is going to make, when I'd be leaving her all day with strangers? I just don't think you could pay someone to be a mom for you.

Before I had her, I thought I'd be able to go to school during the day full-time. Then I had her, and I thought I'd take two classes a day. Then I thought, "Okay, I'll just do one a day, because with the half-hour commute, you're already talking about three hours a day, and then with two hours of studying, that makes five hours."And then I thought, "What's the consequence of that?" It's that the baby would have to be with a sitter five hours a day, five days a week. So she would be the one paying the price for it. And I don't want her to have to do that.

But I can't help thinking about how, during my days at home with Suzy, I'm never doing anything to challenge myself. I never put myself on the line. My own mother worked. We had my grandmother living with us, so I was never left with strangers. And I guess that's part of what gives me the sense that I should be doing something other than just being a mother.

The really ironic thing is that one of the reasons I'm trying to take such good care of Suzy is so that she'll grow up and have all these options I don't think I have. When I see her getting frustrated playing with a toy, I think, "Oh, don't give up! Don't end up like your mother."

"*I Want Gus to Be a Different Kind of Male.*"

Olga is a single mother by choice; the baby's father has seen him several times but isn't involved in their lives on an on-going basis. Unlike Wendy, who fears her child will grow up like her, Olga is a committed feminist, who is extremely conscious of trying to present herself as a positive role-model. To Olga, being a Good Mother includes supporting her family, not only because there's no one else to do that but because she wants to prove something to her son about what women can be.

I'm very proud of the fact that I'm not relying on a man to take care of me. That I'm taking care of my son and myself by myself. My parents have also been very generous; I certainly wouldn't be driving a Volvo if my parents hadn't just said, "Go buy a good used car. Here's the money; pay us back at your leisure." Of course, my brother, who is ten years older than me, owes them the same amount of money and is borrowing more. It says something about our economy that two healthy, able-bodied people like ourselves are being helped by two working-class parents who saved and are now living quite nicely themselves. It's not because my parents were better savers than us, but because the economy is now very different. But then again, my brother and I live very differently. My parents never went out to dinner. They rarely went to a movie. They didn't have child-care expenses, although that's because they worked opposite shifts: he worked days and she worked nights, and they saw each other on weekends. And I think it kept their marriage alive in many ways. They looked forward to their weekends together, and they were very focused on their family. They weren't involved in their careers that were spiraling upwards; they were working-class stiffs who did a job for a wage and were glad to get home.

Anyway, once in a while they send me a hundred bucks, and they helped me with the car, and I know I could count on them in an emergency. But beyond that, I'm proud that I'm supporting myself, and doing it four days a week instead of five so I can spend time with my son. I could work more and make more money, but I just feel these years are too precious and I want three full days a week with him, and as much of the other ones as I can have.

Motherhood has reconfirmed my suspicions that it's mothers who raise children. It seems as though so much is being said about husbands having much more influence in the household, which made me, as a potential single parent, think that my child would really be missing something. But that's not true, from what I can see. From what I can see, I'm missing an income and a sex life, although married women with small children also seem to be missing a sex life.

Not that I haven't seen some nice fathers. But it's women—and if it's not moms, then it's other women—who are raising children in this culture, and if anyone says anything different, they're really kidding themselves.

I want Gus to be a different kind of male. I want him to be his own person, but I want him to filter what the patriarchy will make him be. I want him to balance what he sees in the world with images of lots of competent, caring women, which is what fills his life now: competent, caring, fun, athletic, working women. If I had any worries about that making him "feminine" in some ways, they've been dissipated by seeing how innately not-feminine he is. But maybe most of the women he's around aren't what the culture would call feminine either, in terms of being passive, delicate, quiet. Gus is very active, sometimes aggressive, big and strong. He likes to use his body in strong ways; he loves all kinds of sports; he likes rough-and-tumble play and loud noises. I don't think of any of those things as being the property of men, but they certainly aren't feminine. But I'm all those things, too. I mean, I may not be rough-and-tumble, but I'm not delicate. I'm loud, and

I talk a lot, and I like excitement and fast rides, and I'm not scared by thunderstorms. I want him to be a whole, integrated person who likes to use his body and his mind.

"A Lot of My Thinking Has Been about How You Reconcile Maternal Values with the Insights of What We Call Feminism."

Vera's baby was unplanned, but very much wanted. Going through with the pregnancy meant dropping her career ambitions, at least for the time being, and she and her husband are just keeping the family afloat because he can watch the baby while she works all day, while she takes the baby when he goes to work at night. Like Olga, she is a committed feminist, but she has to struggle to reconcile the theory with the ideas her upbringing implanted in her mind, and her own decision to sacrifice achievement for motherhood. And, like Olga, she thinks that being a Good Mother entails bringing up a child who won't live in a world where women's roles are narrowly defined.

We were graduate students when I got pregnant. We were planning to get married, but we hadn't set a date. We knew we wanted to have kids someday, but not till after we were more settled. But despite our precautions, I got pregnant.

I knew it would be very difficult, that people would think I was crazy for going ahead with it, that my husband and I would have to postpone our plans, that as soon as my parents found out, they'd cut me off. I would have to leave school, not knowing whether a grant would be available when I wanted to go back, and we basically had nothing to live on. But I felt I had to have her. As soon as I realized I was pregnant, I felt very protective of the baby.

I knew that having a child would be a handicap in terms of my achievement, or what is considered in this society to be achievement. But I felt I really had to fight this idea that you achieve or you have children—that ignores the fact that having children is an achievement itself, as worthy as anything you might do with your mind.

And having grown up in what I'd call a dysfunctional family, I really wondered, "Can I treat my own child differently from the way I was treated?" I was a very grubby child. I never learned that I was worthy of taking care of myself. I want my daughter to feel she deserves to look nice—not that she has to perform, but that she has a good sense of herself. I don't want her to feel wicked for asserting herself. And that being dependent on someone doesn't make you a parasite.

I've almost always considered myself a feminist. I come from a very conservative, traditional family, but I always sensed a big difference between what I was told about women and what the experience of being female was. Then I went to a women's college, where there was a strong emphasis on being strong—"like a man." I remember one night being at dinner with about ten other people, and one of my friends remarked, "You know what I'd really like to do now? I'd really like to have a baby." And there was this huge, collective gasp, like, how could anyone aspire to *that*?

But I always knew I wanted to get married and have a baby, and I always felt there was something sexist in the feminism that said there was no inherent value in family life. A lot of my thinking has been about how you reconcile maternal values with the insights of what we call feminism.

I think you can be a mother without sacrificing yourself completely. And you can't be a mother without being tough. It's not something you passively submit to. The phrase "the weaker sex" absolutely outrages me since I've had the baby. How many men do you know who could get through *labor*?

Starting when I was pregnant, I'd be walking in a crowd and I'd start to think, "Every person in here grew inside the body of a woman." But we never talk about that. It's the most basic fact of our existence, and it's unacknowledged.

Because I had a daughter, I think, I want things to be different by the time she has children. I want to teach her that it's a wonderful thing to live in a female body. She really likes looking at books, and I bought one that has pictures of women giving birth, and she's absolutely fascinated by it. I explained about how women grow babies in their stomachs, and then how they come out. And she seemed very concerned that the women might be in pain. So I told her, "It hurts very much, but something good comes out of it. After the pain stops, you have the baby forever."

And then I showed her the picture of the newborn, and she seemed to know just what it was. She nestled her face against the picture. And if I teach her about all this, how valuable it really is, maybe she'll have an easier time of it than I had.

Recommended Reading

American Mom: Motherhood, Politics, and Humble Pie by Mary Kay Blakely. Pocket Books, New York, 1995.

The Feminine Mystique by Betty Friedan. Dell, New York, 1983.

Inventing Motherhood: The Consequences of an Ideal by Ann Dally. Schocken Books, New York, 1983.

Mother's Day is Over: The Realities and Rewards of Motherhood Today by Shirley Rogers Radl. Arbor House, New York, 1987.

Motherself: A Mythic Analysis of Motherhood by Kathryn Allen Rabuzzi. Indiana University Press, Bloomington and Indianapolis, 1988.

The Myths of Motherhood: How Culture Reinvents the Good Mother by Shari L. Thurer. Penguin, New York, 1994.

Of Woman Born: Motherhood as Experience and Institution by Adrienne Rich. Norton, New York, 1995.

Ourselves as Mothers: The Universal Experience of Motherhood by Sheila Kitzinger. Addison-Wesley, Reading, Mass., 1994.